W9-DFT-288

Black Americans of Achievement

LEGACY EDITION

Jamie Foxx

ENTERTAINER

Black Americans of Achievement

LEGACY EDITION

Muhammad Ali
Maya Angelou
Josephine Baker
George Washington Carver
Ray Charles
Johnnie Cochran
Frederick Douglass
W.E.B. Du Bois
Jamie Foxx
Marcus Garvey
Savion Glover
Alex Haley
Jimi Hendrix
Gregory Hines
Langston Hughes
Jesse Jackson
Scott Joplin
Coretta Scott King
Martin Luther King Jr.
Spike Lee
Malcolm X
Bob Marley
Thurgood Marshall
Barack Obama
Jesse Owens
Rosa Parks
Colin Powell
Condoleezza Rice
Chris Rock
Clarence Thomas
Sojourner Truth
Harriet Tubman
Nat Turner
Madam C.J. Walker
Booker T. Washington
Oprah Winfrey
Tiger Woods

Black Americans of Achievement
LEGACY EDITION

Jamie Foxx

ENTERTAINER

Anne M. Todd

CHELSEA HOUSE
PUBLISHERS
An imprint of Infobase Publishing

Jamie Foxx

Copyright © 2008 by Infobase Publishing

Chelsea House
An imprint of Infobase Publishing
132 West 31st Street
New York NY 10001

Library of Congress Cataloging-in-Publication Data

Todd, Anne M.
  Jamie Foxx / Anne M. Todd.
    p. cm. — (Black Americans of achievement, legacy edition)
  Includes bibliographical references and index.
  ISBN 978-1-60413-000-3 (hardcover)
  1. Foxx, Jamie. 2. Actors—United States—Biography. I. Title. II. Series.

  PN2287.F632T63 2008
  791.4302'8092—dc22
  [B]
                          2008008430

Chelsea House books are available at special discounts when purchased in bulk quantities for businesses, associations, institutions, or sales promotions. Please call our Special Sales Department in New York at (212) 967-8800 or (800) 322-8755.

You can find Chelsea House on the World Wide Web at
http://www.chelseahouse.com

Series design by Keith Trego
Cover design by Keith Trego and Jooyoung An

Printed in the United States of America

Bang ML 10 9 8 7 6 5 4 3 2 1

This book is printed on acid-free paper.

All links and web addresses were checked and verified to be correct at the time of publication. Because of the dynamic nature of the web, some addresses and links may have changed since publication and may no longer be valid.

Contents

A Lot to Talk About

On February 27, 2005, the Kodak Theatre in Hollywood, California, was the hottest place to be. On this night, the 77th Annual Academy Awards ceremony, which recognized and honored directors, actors, and writers from the film industry, aired live around the world. The scene was Hollywood glamour at its best. Limousines crowded the streets and fans tried to catch glimpses of their favorite actors. Interviewers and reporters, ready to interview stars as they passed, lined the red carpet. For more than an hour, a stream of celebrities arrived.

When actor, comedian, and songwriter Jamie Foxx stepped onto the red carpet, people took notice. With his shaved head held high, his shoulders back, and his gait confident, Foxx looked like a dazzling all-around winner. Impeccably dressed, Foxx made his way down the carpet with self-assurance and grace. He wore a stunning midnight blue suit with black pinstripes, which was designed and created especially for him by

Jamie Foxx attended the 77th Annual Academy Awards accompanied by his daughter, Corinne. Here, Foxx and Corinne pose together with the Oscar Foxx won that night for his best actor work in *Ray*.

one of London's top designers, Ozwald Boateng. A black-and-white diamond watch; a diamond ring set in platinum; and red, gold, and blue sunglasses with diamond accents completed Foxx's look.

Corinne Marie Foxx, 10 years old at the time, accompanied Foxx to the award show. Alongside her father, Corinne glided down the carpet in a long, flowing white gown with matching white gloves and a diamond headband. She beamed with happiness and pride as the pair stopped every few feet to pose for photos and answer questions.

Along the way, one reporter showed Foxx a live film feed from Terrell High School in Texas, which Foxx had attended as a teenager. On the monitor, Foxx saw friends and fans gathered in the school's Performing Arts Center to show their support. They looked happy and proud, and Foxx was glad to have his hometown standing by to cheer for him. He had come a long way since his youth in Texas. On this night, Foxx was nominated for two Academy Awards: one for his supporting role in the film *Collateral* with Tom Cruise, and the other for his starring role in the film *Ray*, in which Foxx portrays Ray Charles, the legendary rhythm-and-blues (R&B) entertainer.

When the nominations had been announced a few months earlier, Jamie Foxx joined an elite group of actors: He became the tenth person in Academy history to be nominated in two acting categories in the same year. Julianne Moore (2002), Emma Thompson and Holly Hunter (1993), and Al Pacino (1992) are some of the other actors who have received dual nominations. Foxx had also become the second male (Al Pacino was the first) to receive two acting Oscar nominations in the same year for two different movies.

Foxx did not win the Academy Award for his performance in *Collateral*; the supporting actor Oscar went to Morgan Freeman (other nominees were Alan Alda, Thomas Haden Church, and Clive Owen). Nevertheless, the night was one to celebrate: Foxx won an Academy Award for his talented performance as Ray Charles in *Ray*. The competition had been stiff; the other nominees were Don Cheadle for *Hotel Rwanda*, Johnny Depp for *Finding Neverland*, Leonardo DiCaprio for *The Aviator*, and Clint Eastwood for *Million Dollar Baby*.

During Foxx's acceptance speech, he gave special thanks to the woman who had always stood by him and pushed him to follow his dreams: his grandmother, Estelle Talley (some sources refer to her as Esther), who had died only four months earlier. In his heartfelt speech, Foxx told the audience, "[My grandmother, Estelle] still talks to me, only now she talks to me in my dreams. I can't wait to go to sleep tonight. We've got a lot to talk about."

Bradshaw Street Community

Eric Marlon Bishop was born on December 13, 1967, in the small town of Terrell, Texas, in Kaufman County. (Eric would not change his name to Jamie Foxx until 1989.) Terrell's rough terrain, like the rest of the Lone Star State, is flat. The gently rolling plains and rocky soil extend as far as the eye can see. Summers in Terrell are hot and winters are mild, which are the perfect growing conditions for cotton, the town's major contribution to the economy during the early 1900s.

The town of Terrell has its origins in the late 1800s. In 1872, the Texas and Pacific Railroad Company had formed plans for an extensive railroad. The new transcontinental line was to begin in Longview, Texas, and stretch west to California. When the plans changed to route the train through Dallas, located 32 miles (51.5 kilometers) east of present-day Terrell, land surveyor Robert A. Terrell approached the railroad company with a proposition: Terrell offered to donate 100 acres of his own land in exchange for a depot on the rail line. In 1873, the railroad agreed to the proposition, construction began, and a railway line began to take shape through the center of the newly created town. By 1875, Terrell's population was about 1,000. When Eric Bishop was born in 1967, Terrell's population had reached approximately 12,000.

CHILDHOOD DAYS

Eric Bishop spent only a short time with his biological parents. Eric's biological mother, Louise Annette, was the adopted daughter of Mark and Estelle Talley. Louise Annette was a teenager when she married Eric's father, Darrel Bishop. Soon after, she became pregnant with Eric. The young, inexperienced couple had a rocky relationship, and once Eric was born, they quickly realized they were not ready to take on the emotional or financial responsibilities of parenthood. Louise Annette and Darrel handed Eric over to Louise's parents and left Terrell without looking back. Baby Eric was seven months old.

Mark and Estelle Talley, who were already in their sixties, adopted seven-month-old Eric, which made Eric's biological mother his sister and his biological grandmother his mother, according to law. The Talleys had always worked hard to ensure a safe and happy life for themselves and their children. In addition to Eric, the Talleys would later care for Eric's two half sisters.

Both Estelle and Mark Talley worked for wealthy white families across town. Estelle cleaned house and Mark cared for a yard and garden. Sometimes the families called them back to work extra hours, demanding that Estelle and Mark drop whatever they were doing and get to work, whether at five in the morning or nine at night. Although Eric admired his grandparents' strong work ethic, it both angered and saddened him to see the white employers treat his family with so little respect. This raw experience planted the seeds of determination to do something more with his life.

Jamie Foxx, then known as Eric Marlon Bishop, grew up in the small town of Terrell, Texas, east of Dallas. This is a 2005 photograph of downtown Terrell, looking east down West Moore Avenue.

The black community of Bradshaw Street, where the Talleys lived, looked out for one another and one another's children. Eric and his siblings grew up in a strict household where physical punishments were used to enforce order. The Talleys and their extended family expected children to behave and stay out of trouble. Even while Mark and Estelle were at work, aunts, grandmothers, friends, and neighbors were ready to look after the children and hand out any needed discipline. Most everyone shared the common goals in rearing the African-American youth of Bradshaw Street, which were to teach responsibility and emphasize education. During the summer months, Estelle herself would gather the neighborhood children together in the Talley's small yellow house to teach them to read. Under Estelle's watchful eye and guidance, all the children in the neighborhood got an early start on their education.

The Bradshaw Street community relied on one another for basics, such as food or clothing, as well as for parenting help. It was difficult for African Americans in Terrell to get jobs. The Talleys were poor, with only a few possessions; nevertheless, the community was rich with love and unity. It was a cooperative village in which everyone laughed together, played together, worked together, struggled together, and attended church together. The people of the Bradshaw Street community realized they had to depend on each other to help see everyone through hard times.

MUSIC AND RELIGION

Estelle decided to teach Eric to play the piano when he was just three years old, and he learned easily. She saw something special in Eric that she wanted to nurture, so when Eric turned five, Estelle signed him up for piano lessons from a professional teacher. Although they had little money, Estelle thought

IN HIS OWN WORDS…

In an interview, talk-show host Oprah Winfrey asked Jamie Foxx if he thought all people are created equal. He responded, "No. If that were true, there'd be no poverty, no shortcomings. . . . We're all energy. Some people are stronger forces than others."

the lessons were essential. She hoped to see young Eric Bishop succeed in life and realized that his exceptional piano playing might help him rise in the world.

Eric quickly developed a deep passion for music. The study of music helped Eric's reading and memory, which in turn helped him to excel academically in school. He also discovered that he loved to sing. As a young boy, Eric sang in the church choir, which had about 25 members. Eric liked to stand up in

Pianos and Pianists

Standard pianos have 88 keys. When pressed, these keys control felt hammers that strike steel strings to create a sound. A piano also has three pedals for the pianist's foot: the damper pedal (on the right) causes all the keys to vibrate, which enriches the piano's tone; the sostenuto pedal (in the middle) makes it possible to sustain some notes while the player's hands are free to play other notes; and the soft pedal (on the left) causes a muted, or softened, sound. Pianos come in upright (vertical) styles or they can be grand (horizontal).

Bartolomeo Cristofori made the first piano around 1700. The modern piano that we know today did not become popular until the mid 1700s. At first, people used the piano primarily as an accompaniment to singing or as one of the instruments in an ensemble for chamber music. The player piano, which contains a mechanism by which the instrument generates notes automatically, was developed in the late 1800s.

A few of the classical and jazz pianists who made their mark in the 1970s while Eric was growing up included Ruth Laredo, Oscar Peterson, and Nina Simone. Ruth Laredo was one of the first celebrated American women pianists and was known for her recordings of the music of another famous pianist, Sergei Rachmaninoff. Oscar Peterson, born in Canada, became a well-known jazz pianist, winning seven Grammy awards between the years of 1974 and 1991. Nina Simone, an African American who came from a large, poor family, went on to play at the Juilliard School during her senior year of high school. Simone created a distinctive piano style that incorporated her many musical interests: jazz, classical, blues, and folk. She recorded almost 60 albums. Comedian Richard Pryor commented, "White people had Judy Garland; black people had Nina [Simone]."

front of the congregation and sing. Music teacher Doris Johnson gave Eric voice lessons and taught him music appreciation, where he learned about the elements, forms, styles, and periods of music.

New Hope Baptist Church was an important part of Eric's childhood. He and his family spent a great deal of time there, usually attending several days each week. The church brought the Bradshaw Street community together for direction, comfort, prayer, and inspiration. Terrell had few entertainment options for young people, but at church, children found things to do, including taking music lessons and just hanging out together to talk and have fun. The other kids thought Eric was funny and enjoyed listening to his jokes and watching him act silly. Sometimes Eric would mimic a teacher, a relative, or someone he had seen on television, and his friends would laugh and laugh. Having watched the church's preacher capture the attention of the congregation so fully each day, Eric learned the best ways to use his own tone of voice and body language to deliver his point most effectively. Eric would later describe church as his primary learning ground for everything. Church was where he learned to appreciate music, heard new jokes, and even met girls.

By age 13, Eric was already earning money as the music director of his church choir. The extra income could have benefited the entire family, but Estelle insisted that Eric save the money he earned. She was always thinking of her son's future and realized the savings could help him if he ever decided to leave Terrell. The experience of directing the choir taught Eric about punctuality, responsibility, and leadership. It also helped to teach him about following through with directions. As director, Eric had to listen to what the preacher and the congregation wanted from the choir, make the necessary adjustments, and deliver. Around this time, Eric also learned to play the drums, trumpet, and baritone. Music and religious study took

Eric Bishop and his family connected with their community through the New Hope Baptist Church, shown above. Eric learned a lot about music at the church, where he was the music director for the choir and played the piano to accompany them.

up much of his time, but he also participated in Boy Scouts and sports.

Eric's birth parents, Louise Annette and Darrel, had moved away to Dallas. Darrel eventually converted to Islam, changed his name to Shahid Abdulah, and became a stockbroker. What had started as a rocky relationship remained so, and the couple divorced in 1974, when Eric was six years old. The divorce had little effect on Eric, however, because he was not living with them and had no relationship with either parent. Louise Annette later married George Dixon, with whom she had two daughters. Although Eric's birth parents both returned to Terrell on occasion, they rarely spent any quality time with Eric. In stark contrast to the lack of affection and care from his birth parents, Eric's upbringing with Mark and Estelle Talley was brimming with love and support.

Church and music filled much of Eric's time as a young boy. At home and at church, piano playing and singing were a daily part of his life. He exhibited natural talents for both. He also made new discoveries: He realized that he liked to make people laugh, he liked to perform, and he liked to be in front of an audience. In addition, he had a knack for mimicking people, which friends and family found highly entertaining. As Eric moved forward in his life, he began to realize that humor, like music, would always be something he treasured.

3

Teenage Years

Estelle Talley was proud of Eric's work and involvement with the church and his dedication to the choir. She also wanted Eric to get work outside the church, and by the time Eric had reached his teenage years, Estelle was busy helping Eric obtain musical gigs in Terrell's swanky white neighborhoods. It was not easy to get to these gigs, and it entailed something Eric preferred to avoid: crossing into the neighborhoods on the other side of the railroad tracks.

The railroad tracks that split the town of Terrell in half did more than divide the town geographically; they also divided the town racially. This kind of segregation still filled the South in the 1970s and 1980s. Eric knew to stay on his side of the tracks, where black people primarily lived. When he crossed over, white people were likely to call him names and treat him disrespectfully. White children once chased Eric down a street, threatening him with what turned out to be fake guns. On the "black side" of the tracks, white people rarely made appearances. Eric felt safer in his own neighborhood, where he had the acceptance of people who cared for him—his family and his community.

LIFE LESSONS

The treatment of blacks as second-class citizens was the result of the haunting spirit of Jim Crow laws, which had passed in the United States between the mid 1800s and the mid 1960s. These state laws had legalized segregation and discrimination toward blacks. They prevented blacks and whites from doing all kinds of things together, such as attending the same schools, using the same bathrooms, riding in the same train compartment, eating at the same restaurant, or sitting side by side at a movie theater. The U.S. Congress finally put an end to Jim Crow laws in 1964 when it passed the Civil Rights Act, which outlawed discrimination in public accommodations (such as hotels, restaurants, and theaters) and in employment. The following year, Congress passed the Voting Rights Act, which gave all people, regardless of race or color, an equal opportunity to vote. Both acts stopped states from creating state laws that could legalize segregation.

Despite the changes in law, black Americans still suffered from the years of prejudice and intolerance, which lingered in places all over America, including small-town Terrell. When Eric crossed the tracks to play the music gigs Estelle had set up, he was vulnerable to ill treatment and putdowns. For example, one year when Eric was about 15 years old, he arrived at a white family's estate to play the piano for a Christmas party. Eric had no driver's license yet, so his 16-year-old friend (also African American) had driven Eric to the party. The two boys rang the bell at the fancy southern mansion. When the white owner came to the door, he asked what was going on, and Eric explained that he was there to play the piano. The man asked why his friend had come along and, after Eric explained, the

The house above is Estelle Talley's home in Terrell, Texas. Estelle and her husband adopted Eric Bishop, their grandson, and raised him as their own.

man told Eric he could not have two black people in his home at one time. He would not allow Eric's friend to wait outside in the yard, either; he had to be completely off the white man's property.

After Eric's friend left (planning to return for Eric after the party), the white man saw that Eric was not wearing a tuxedo, so he gave him a tuxedo jacket to wear while he performed. At the end of the night, when Eric tried to return the jacket, the man said he could never wear it again after a black person had, so he told Eric he might as well keep it. He also instructed Eric to wait for his friend to pick him up away from the house and grounds, on the side of the road.

This kind of painful lesson taught Eric about people's prejudice and hate. He understood how deeply certain people felt hate. Nevertheless, Estelle believed that the exposure to harsh realities had its benefits. She wanted Eric to see firsthand that, as an African American, he would have to work harder and endure more to make something of himself. Estelle also wanted Eric to see the tremendous value his music could be to him. It would give him the chance to make a living for himself doing something he loved instead of cleaning houses or working in yards.

Mark and Estelle loved Eric deeply and did what they thought would help guide him to become a strong, honest man—a real "southern gentleman." Estelle desperately wanted Eric to have more choices and opportunities than she and Mark had in their lives. She taught Eric to walk tall, with his shoulders back and his head held high. More important, Estelle told him to be proud and confident, and Mark reminded Eric not to play a hero, but always to be a man. With Mark and Estelle's guidance, Eric learned to respect himself and carefully consider the choices he made.

Throughout Eric's childhood, he eagerly awaited the occasional brief visits of his biological parents, Abdulah and Louise Annette. Since Abdulah and Eric both loved sports, Eric would have had fun playing with his father. Eric longed for attention from his mother, who was beautiful and, now that she was living in nearby Dallas, sophisticated. Unfortunately, his parents frequently failed to show up when they promised. Abdulah, who still practiced Islam, did not approve of Eric's dedication to the Baptist Church. As a result, he found it hard to be around Eric and wanted little to do with him. Louise Annette had her own life—one that did not include young Eric. Even as an adult, Eric would have little contact with either of his biological parents.

SCHOOL DAYS

At school, Eric was a good student and excelled in his classes. He paid attention in class, studied, and did his homework. In addition to being smart, Eric knew how to be funny and he loved to entertain his classmates. The teachers at his school knew how much the other students liked to watch Eric perform. When he was in second grade, Eric's teacher would tell the students that Eric would perform if the class finished their work and were well behaved. As a result of the teacher's promised reward, both the teacher and the students were happy: The students did well, and Eric entertained, eventually turning his classroom act into his own show called "An Afternoon with Eric Bishop."

As a teenager, Eric played quarterback for his high school football team, the Terrell Tigers. Eric worked hard for the Tigers, and he became a star on the field. The Dallas newspaper noticed his efforts, and the attention and praise he received made Eric wonder if he should consider football as a possible career. He spent time envisioning himself as the next up-and-coming quarterback for his favorite football team, the Dallas Cowboys.

Eric was a natural and gifted athlete who enjoyed playing the game. Yet despite Eric's abilities, he did not fully embrace football in Texas. The community, the school, and even the church pressured Eric to excel in the sport and help earn Terrell High School a championship. In one championship game, Eric heard the preacher of his church boo him from the stands after Eric threw the ball out of bounds to avoid an interception. Eric realized that the traditions and the expectations attached to Terrell football were intense and extreme, and he was not sure he felt the same passion for football that was apparent in the Terrell community. Nonetheless, he stuck with it through high school and still enjoyed the game (and he would remain a huge Dallas Cowboys fan).

In addition to football, Eric played tennis and ran track in high school, excelling at all three. Fellow Terrell High student Cynthea Rhodes (now Cynthea Rhodes-Patterson) was also an ace on the track. She and Eric both qualified for state championships. After high school, Rhodes went on to earn a degree from the University of Texas and then join the 1996

On the Terrell High School track team, one of Eric's teammates was Cynthea Rhodes, who went on to run track at the University of Texas at Austin. In 1996, Rhodes competed to join the U.S. Olympic track team. She is shown here landing the triple jump with which she won the women's finals, thus earning a place on the 1996 Olympic team.

U.S. Olympic team as a triple jumper. She was also a member of the World Championship Teams in 1993, 1995, and 1997.

Although Eric loved running with the football, racing across the tennis court to return a serve, and sprinting down that last bend of the track to the finish line, he also loved the down times—especially making his teammates laugh in the locker room with his latest impersonation or relaying a joke he had heard in church. Robert Daniels, Eric's track coach in high school, would later tell the *Dallas Examiner*, "[Eric] was an outgoing kid, always impersonating somebody. If he saw you, he could impersonate you."

Sports and jokes aside, when Eric focused on how he wanted to spend his life, it always involved music. At one school talent competition in which Eric sang, the girls in the audience moved toward the front of the room to be closer to Eric the moment he started to perform onstage. Eric loved how his music affected the girls, so he put together two R&B bands when he was a teenager: One was called Leather and Lace, and the other was called Excalibur.

Leather and Lace reflected the influence of musician Prince, who had opened new doors in the music world in 1980 with his album *Dirty Mind*. In 1983, Prince sold more than 3 million copies of his hit album *1999*. Then, in 1984, the soundtrack to his film *Purple Rain* sold more than 10 million copies in the United States alone, making Prince a superstar. Eric was both impressed and inspired by the way Prince combined elements of R&B, funk, and soul with pop, rock, and jazz.

When interviewed years later, Jamie Foxx admitted that Leather and Lace was not very good; they performed onstage only once. Similarly, Eric's other R&B band, Excalibur, did not meet his expectations and was equally short-lived. Although the bands were not successful, the experience showed Eric what it takes to put a band together, how a band works, and what makes a band succeed or fail.

When Eric was not at school or playing in a band, he liked to hang out and relax with friends, like Gilbert Willie and Torrez Thomas; in fact, the three of them are still friends today. The boys liked to play basketball and football together, as well as music. They also liked to work on comedy routines, try out new jokes, and show each other their impersonations of celebrities.

Like many teenagers, Eric loved to watch television, and he found inspiration in popular shows of the time, such as *Sanford and Son* (starring Redd Foxx, Demond Wilson, and

LaWanda Page), *All in the Family* (starring Carroll O'Connor, Jean Stapleton, Rob Reiner, and Sally Struthers), *Taxi* (starring Judd Hirsch, Danny DeVito, Marilu Henner, and Tony Danza), *Barney Miller* (starring Hal Linden, Max Gail, and Ron Glass), and *The Bob Newhart Show* (starring Bob Newhart, Suzanne Pleshette, Peter Bonerz, and Marcia Wallace). Some of his favorite television entertainers were Richard Pryor, Carol Burnett, Flip Wilson, and Redd Foxx. Eric spent long hours watching his idols, studying their delivery and individual nuances, and working to impersonate them in detail.

In 1984, Eric had the chance to see his first big concert. He traveled with some friends to Texas Stadium, in Dallas, for the Jackson's Victory Tour. More than 2 million people attended the Jackson's tour, which consisted of 55 concerts. The Jackson brothers included Michael, Jermaine, Tito, Randy, Marlon, and Jackie (who had a knee injury and only performed at one concert). At the final concert of the tour, Michael Jackson announced his split from the Jacksons; he would continue as a solo artist.

At the time, Michael Jackson was a huge star, and Eric was mesmerized and awestruck at the show. He witnessed people

IN HIS OWN WORDS...

In an interview with Neil Gladstone, Jamie Foxx talked about black stereotypes. He told Gladstone,

> I think *Sanford and Son* and *All in the Family* were the funniest TV shows I've ever seen. What's so funny is that they're real. Redd Foxx was this broke black dude who worked in a junkyard, but he had so much dignity and was proud of his junk and that's what I think is real.... Archie Bunker was a bigot. Those are the things you laugh at because they're real. Stereotypes are funny. I like fried chicken, loud music and fast cars—but to treat me bad because I like those things is the problem.

around him pass out when Michael Jackson stepped onto the stage and started to sing, "Wanna Be Startin' Somethin'." Eric and his friends had seats close to the stage, where Eric could see firsthand the passion and intensity with which Michael Jackson sang. Eric Bishop could easily relate to these feelings.

Sad times were to come for Eric. His grandfather and adopted father, Mark Talley, became ill and died in 1985, when

Richard Pryor

When Jamie Foxx watched television as a child, he admired Richard Pryor, whom many considered to be a comic genius. Pryor, born on December 1, 1940, had a rough childhood. He started his stand-up comedy career in 1960 and, over time, he developed a unique sense of humor and commanding stage presence. Pryor was daring and uninhibited. He took chances with comedy, yet he kept it authentic and honest. As Jamie Foxx did in the 1980s and 1990s, many young, hopeful comedians still study Pryor's stand-up routines to learn about timing, delivery, and content.

In addition to stand-up comedy, Pryor also branched out into other areas of the entertainment industry. He appeared in nearly 50 movies, including *The Busy Body* (1967), *Lady Sings the Blues* (1972), *Car Wash* (1976), *The Muppet Movie* (1979), *Superman III* (1983), *Harlem Nights* (1989), and *Lost Highway* (1997). On television, Pryor starred in *The Richard Pryor Show* and a children's show called *Pryor's Place*, among others. He was also a guest host of the late-night comedy show *Saturday Night Live*.

Pryor was diagnosed with multiple sclerosis (MS), a degenerative disease of the central nervous system, in 1986. He suffered a heart attack in his home on December 10, 2005, and he died later that day at the hospital, just a few days after his sixty-fifth birthday. During his career, Pryor opened the door to a richer, more honest form of comedy that dug down and brought insight to topics never before broached by comedians. He remains an inspiration to aspiring comedians. As Damon Wayans says in the liner notes in *Richard Pryor: And It's Deep Too! The Complete Warner Bros. Recordings (1968–1992)*, "By telling the truth about his pain, Richard held up a mirror to society, and we were able to see our fears, our beauty, our prejudice, our wretchedness, our hopes, our dreams—all of our contradictions. [Richard Pryor] is truly the greatest comedian of our time."

Eric was 17 years old. Mark had taken Eric into his home and adopted him as his own son after Eric's biological father left him. Mark had offered Eric a family, security, support, and love at a time when he might have had none. The death was difficult for Eric, who was with Mark during his last hours. When Mark first stopped breathing, Eric performed CPR on him, but he was unable to revive his grandfather. Mark's death was especially hard on Estelle; she and Mark had persevered through good times and bad. Afterwards, Eric felt that he had to contribute more to his family, and he felt an even stronger desire to show Estelle that he could do well in life.

In June 1986, Eric Bishop accepted his diploma with a smile and a great deal of satisfaction as he became an official graduate of Terrell High School. Although the football pressures had sometimes weighed him down, he would look back on his high school days fondly. He had enjoyed joking around with his friends, and he was proud that the effort and time he put into his studies had allowed him to succeed and excel in academics. Estelle beamed with pride and fulfillment at Eric's graduation ceremony; her desire to see Eric Bishop succeed in life and follow his dreams was that much closer to fruition. Eric's birthparents, however, did not attend.

4

Life Beyond Terrell

Upon graduating from high school, Eric Bishop was ready and eager to say good-bye to small-town Terrell, Texas, and see what else the world had to offer him. It was much more difficult for him to say good-bye to Estelle, who had been his strongest supporter thus far. Although he was struggling with the idea of moving away, Estelle encouraged him to follow his dreams and become a musician. She believed that his classical and gospel beginnings would give him a solid base on which to build his formal piano training. Estelle thought that he would be able to find a job as an accompanist, a musical director, or perhaps a piano teacher. She would proudly follow Bishop's career, and she would continue to be his biggest admirer and supporter.

So Bishop prepared to leave behind the only home he had ever known to attend United States International University (USIU) (now named Alliant International University) in San Diego.

He had received a full classical piano scholarship based on the praise he had received for playing the piano for his church choir at New Hope Baptist Church. Now, with his mind made up, Bishop left Texas and headed west to Southern California.

NEW DIRECTIONS

From 1986 to 1988, Bishop studied classical piano and music theory with Russian teachers at USIU's School of Visual and Performing Arts. Students at this liberal arts college benefited from highly trained teachers, small class sizes, and a world-wide perspective. USIU campuses were found throughout the United States and the world. Bishop attended the Scripps Ranch campus, located in San Diego, California. The classes that Bishop took there allowed him to enrich and develop the classical piano training he had already received.

The diversity of Scripps Ranch campus amazed Bishop, and he enjoyed meeting people from all over the world who had come to study music. In Terrell, the majority of people were white or black, but here on campus, Bishop met people from Africa, South America, and Europe. He learned about different cultures and customs. Later, when he was known as Jamie Foxx, he would tell the *Sunday Times*, "College was like a haven to me. You'd be exhausted even trying to be racist at the university because there were students from 81 different nations. Racism wasn't in my face in California, like it was in Texas." In college, Bishop started to see that not all people discriminated against blacks. He learned that blacks and whites could be friends; most importantly, he learned they could be equals.

At USIU, Bishop spent long hours playing the piano. Professor Emeritus Jack Tygett, a noted choreographer, actor, and director, headed the Musical Theater department at the time. He enjoyed listening to Bishop play, and he was impressed with his wide range of piano abilities: Bishop could play symphonic music, ragtime, or the latest hit from mainstream music. Bishop also had the opportunity to work with Professor Tygett in some of the university's theatrical productions.

When Bishop wanted time away from campus, he ventured out into the surrounding city of San Diego. In downtown San Diego, he discovered the Comedy Store, a traveling show from Los Angeles where comedians performed stand-up routines. Bishop felt at home listening to the comedians and being around the performers and nightclub atmosphere, and he started to spend more and more of his free time at comedy clubs.

To earn money for food and other living expenses in college, Bishop played piano as the accompanist for the performing arts department's ballet, modern dance, and jazz classes. It was easy to get work because the school offered such a great number of dance classes. The broad background and intensive training Bishop was receiving at USIU was just what he needed to set his musical career in motion.

For his twenty-first birthday, Bishop visited Los Angeles, California, and he loved the upbeat mood of the city. The bright lights, happy people, sunshine, and palm trees felt good and felt right. While there, he and his friends went to a comedy club during an open-mic night. When a friend dared him to get on stage, Bishop's impromptu routine was a crowd pleaser. He thrived on the crowd's appreciation and the way he felt onstage. Soon after this Los Angeles visit, Bishop realized that he wanted to change the course of his career. He soon decided that, instead of making a living as a classical musician, his true passion was to become a music superstar.

Once Bishop fully thought out his new dream, he did not waste any time. He dropped out of college, forgoing his under-graduate degree in fine arts. Although he had learned a lot from USIU and would miss his instructors and campus life, he was also very excited about his revised plan for his future and was eager to set it in action. Bishop packed up his belongings and moved to Los Angeles.

In Los Angeles, Bishop took on a whole new look. He restyled his hair in large curls, similar to the popular R&B/contemporary ballad singer Lionel Richie. In 1982, Richie had released his first solo album, *Lionel Richie*, and it had sold more than 4 million copies. In 1983, he released *Can't Slow Down*, which won the 1984 Grammy for Album of the Year and made Richie a superstar. With Bishop's new look and his confidence in his piano and vocal expertise, he was ready to become the next Lionel Richie. He admired Richie's smooth sound when he sang, and he liked how women reacted to Richie's music. Bishop thought he could have that same effect and popularity, and he wanted to combine his love for singing, playing the piano, and being onstage in front of an audience. Bishop was ready to find a record label willing to produce his music. The time had come for Bishop to become a star.

It did not take long for Bishop to realize that it would be more difficult to get started in the music industry than he had expected. No one was willing to take a risk on this unknown singer from Terrell, Texas. With no entertainment connections and no record deal on the horizon, Bishop had to find other means by which to pay his rent and buy his food. Bishop took a job as a shoe salesperson at Thom McCann, a store in a strip mall. While working there, he saw many other hopeful musicians working in Los Angeles, just like him. He also noticed that hardly any signed with a record company. They ended up in dead-end jobs and gave up on their dreams.

Bishop did not want to end up like that, and he definitely did not imagine himself remaining a shoe salesperson, so he decided to draw upon the talent he had honed during his school days in Terrell, Texas: doing impressions. He already had a routine that he had begun in "An Afternoon with Eric Bishop." Reinvigorated, he decided to take on the Los Angeles comedy scene. Bishop did not intend to completely turn his back on his dream of becoming a music superstar, however; he planned to revisit that idea later.

FROM MUSICIAN TO FUNNY MAN

Bishop diligently made the rounds to open-mic nights at the comedy clubs, and he gave each of the club owners his name: Eric Bishop. Many other young comedians, hoping to get discovered, also made the rounds of open-mic nights and gave their names. Bishop quickly noticed that there were more men than women on the comedy club owners' lists of potential comedians. Club owners, however, wanted to mix up the men and women in order to add variety to the show. As a result, nearly all the female names from the list performed, along with an equal number of males. This gave Bishop an idea. In 1989, Bishop changed his name to Jamie Foxx. He chose this stage name because "Jamie" could be mistaken for a woman on a list of names. The change was a savvy move. He got called to the stage.

Once Foxx began to perform onstage, club owners took notice. They saw a comedian with stage presence, self-confidence, and charm. Shortly thereafter, Foxx started to book regular jobs as a stand-up performer, and soon he was working seven nights a week. His act often included impersonations of such celebrities as comedian Bill Cosby, former president Ronald Regan, politician Jesse Jackson, and Nation of Islam leader Louis Farrakhan—just as he had done in Terrell for his friends and classmates. Crowds loved the act, and they loved Jamie Foxx.

With each performance, Foxx further developed his stage style to display his confidence, sass, energy, and wit. He chose

DID YOU KNOW?

Jamie Foxx chose his last name as a tribute to Redd Foxx, one of his childhood idols. Redd Foxx, nicknamed the "King of Comedy," was best known for his starring role on the television sitcom *Sanford and Son*. Jamie Foxx thought the name "Foxx" would immediately make people think "funny," so it seemed like a good stage name for the up-and-coming comedian.

Redd Foxx (1922–1991), shown above in 1973, was a comedian best known for his starring role in *Sanford and Son*. As
a child, Eric Bishop had idolized Foxx and so chose his last
name to honor the comedian.

his material based on his audiences, noticing that some audiences preferred one kind of material, and certain audiences
preferred another. As Foxx figured out the best way to please
his audiences and fine-tune his presentation, his comedy
steadily improved.

In 1991, Foxx decided to enter the Bay Area Black Comedy Competition and Festival (BABCCF). Held in Oakland, California, the competition gives black comedians from the United

Los Angeles Comedy Clubs

For two years, Foxx made the rounds at many of the comedy clubs in Los Angeles, California. Some of the most famous comedy clubs include:

- **THE COMEDY STORE:** One of Los Angeles's oldest clubs, located on Sunset Strip, the Comedy Store has been around since 1972, when comedian Sammy Shore opened it with Rudy De Luca. In June 1973, when Mitzi Shore took over, she started the first "all stand-up" comedian show. The list of Comedy Store alumni is long and includes greats like Sandra Bernhard, George Carlin, Whoopi Goldberg, Arsenio Hall, Dave Letterman, Eddie Murphy, Chris Tucker, and Robin Williams.

- **THE IMPROV:** Located on Melrose Avenue, the Improv is both a comedy club and dinner theater. It was first founded in New York City in 1963, and opened its Los Angeles branch in 1974. Jim Carrey, Jay Leno, Bette Midler, Eddy Murphy, Richard Pryor, and Lily Tomlin all worked at the Improv as they made their way into comedy.

- **THE LAUGH FACTORY:** This world-famous club is on the corner of Sunset and Laurel. Richard Pryor was one of the first comedians to appear on the Laugh Factory's stage in 1979. Almost all of the great comedians have performed there, including Jim Carrey, Rodney Dangerfield, Red Foxx, George Lopez, Chris Rock, Jerry Seinfeld, Damon Wayans, and Robin Williams. The Laugh Factory personally selects comedians for individual private parties held in its Main Room.

- **THE GROUNDLINGS THEATER:** The Groundlings Theater got its start in 1974, but it made its home in its current location in 1979. Now located in West Hollywood, many *Saturday Night Live* actors got their start here. Alumni for this comedy club include Will Ferrell, Kathy Griffin, Phil Hartman, Lisa Kudrow, and Julia Sweeney.

States and all over the world an opportunity to display their stand-up routines. It has helped young people get started in their comedic careers and have a chance to make connections with people in the entertainment industry. Even with all the young talent present, Foxx won, which gave a huge boost to his resume. Other BABCCF alumni include Chris Tucker, Mike Epps, D.L. Hughley, Sheryl Underwood, and Katt Williams.

IN LIVING COLOR

Foxx was making it as a comedian in California, and he was getting noticed. One evening, while he was performing at a Los Angeles comedy club, Keenen Ivory Wayans, the creator of the popular short-sketch comedy show *In Living Color*, was watching from the audience. Wayans liked Foxx's stage presence and his natural comedic abilities. He thought Foxx would make a nice addition to his show, and he invited him to audition for a spot on *In Living Color*. Always eager to try new things and keep his material fresh, Foxx eagerly tried out for the show. He landed the job and joined the cast during its third season. From October 1991 to February 1994, Foxx worked on the program with other rising stars like Jim Carrey, Tommy Davidson, David Alan Grier, and the younger Wayans siblings, Damon, Kim, Shawn, and Marlon.

Foxx would later call his time on *In Living Color* a training ground that would shape him as an actor. On the set, Foxx made a big impression in a blond wig and lipstick with his character named Wanda. Like the other actors on the show, Foxx worked to create real characters. It was not only about delivering jokes; he wanted to create an entire character that could pull off different feelings and reactions. In addition to Wanda, some of his more memorable characters included Ace, Carl "the Tooth" Williams, Larry, and T-Dog Jenkins.

Just as Estelle Talley had insisted that Foxx work hard and push himself to improve, even when he thought he was at his best, *In Living Color* had a similar effect on Foxx. Keenen Ivory

Wayans was hard on his African-American actors. He ran a tight ship and he let people know when he disapproved of their actions. Wayans knew that African Americans were still not treated equally in the entertainment business, and he wanted to teach Foxx and the other cast members the power of impeccable professionalism. When the actors eventually left the show and went on to work for someone else, they would have the knowledge they needed to stay on good terms with their employers.

Wayans paid attention to all aspects of professionalism. If Foxx arrived late for work—even just five minutes—Wayans pulled him aside and gave him a lecture on the importance of punctuality. Once, Foxx showed up to work wearing the same clothes he had worn the day before, and Wayans again pulled him aside and told him he just could not do that on his set—he had to be constantly aware of his personal appearance. Wayans wanted Foxx to realize that he could never succeed in such a competitive business if he was mediocre or even just coasting. He would have to be a standout, not only in his acting and performance, but in all aspects of the business.

Foxx appreciated the advice, and he regarded Wayans as both a friend and a mentor. Always the good student, Foxx knew how to watch and listen. He also learned a lot from Jim Carrey, who had such an original take on comedy that Foxx never tired of watching him. This helped Foxx absorb all the talent around him, study it, and try to create something new for himself, always seeking to improve upon his own sketches. All of Foxx's hard work and effort paid off: As his art continued to evolve and develop, he became a better comedian.

As a result of *In Living Color*, Foxx became better known in Los Angeles, and he clearly liked the attention. He bought a convertible and enjoyed the Los Angeles nightlife after his hard day's work. Foxx liked to party with his friends, staying out late at nightclubs. Although he quickly took to the glitz and glamour of Hollywood, Foxx still had some small-town Terrell traits and habits. For instance, when he received a check from the studio, he did not deposit it into a bank account; instead, he cashed it and carried the wad of hundred-dollar bills around in his pockets. If he received a check from the show, but he did not need the money right away, he put the check in his closet. Nevertheless, Foxx gradually settled into his new life and started to adjust to city living. He soon felt comfortable and confident both on and off the set.

During Foxx's stint on *In Living Color*, he earned a guest role on a television series called *Roc*, starring Charles Dutton and directed by Stan Lathan. On the show, Foxx played Crazy George in six episodes that aired between December 1992 and November 1993. That year, *Roc* was nominated for an Emmy, which is an annual award given by the Academy of Television Arts and Sciences for prime-time television programs.

The success of Foxx's television shows led to other work, as well. Foxx appeared in his first movie when he landed a minor role in the 1992 film *Toys*, starring Robin Williams, Michael Gambon, and Joan Cusack. *Toys* was directed by Barry Levinson, who had previously directed *Rain Man* in 1988, *Avalon* in 1990, and *Bugsy* in 1991. The Academy of Motion Picture Arts and Sciences nominated *Toys* for two Oscars: Best Art Direction-Set Decoration and Best Costume Design. Although the critics may have appreciated the set designs, costumes, and special effects of *Toys*, the plot and direction were strongly criticized.

In 1993, Foxx starred in his own comedy/music HBO special called *Jamie Foxx: Straight From the Foxxhole*. HBO was known for taking risks with up-and-coming, cutting-edge comedians, and this was a real break for him. The concert program was filmed at the Spreckels Theatre in San Diego, California. Other comedy acts who have performed there include the now-famous Tim Allen, Tommy Davidson, Ellen Degeneres, and George Lopez.

The *Foxxhole* special gave Foxx the opportunity to perform a wide range of his comedy material. He did the impersonations

Foxx got his first big break when Keenan Wayans brought him on as a regular on the comedy sketch show *In Living Color*. Here, Foxx is shown (center) with the other members of the cast. Jim Carrey (top row, second from left), was another actor on the show who went on to bigger roles.

his fans expected, like Bill Cosby and Mike Tyson, always placing the characters in outrageous situations. When he did impersonations of Michael Jackson and Prince, Jamie was able to incorporate dance moves that mimicked them perfectly. The show also included a stand-up routine that the audience loved. At one point in the show, Foxx sat at a grand piano, set up on the right side of the stage, where he played a number of songs—some with silly lyrics and others that were serious. Although *Jamie Foxx: Straight From the Foxxhole* received mixed reviews, it helped to increase Foxx's name recognition and to showcase his musical range and talent.

When Foxx left *In Living Color,* he continued to do stand-up comedy in and around Los Angeles at hot spots like the Comedy Store. He soon discovered, however, that, now that he had left the show, he had lost some prominence in the comedy scene. The change seemed to happen overnight. One night, after a disappointing performance at a club, he heard the crowd roaring with laughter at the comedian who followed him. When Foxx peeked back inside to see who was getting the favorable response, he saw a skinny young black man onstage, who turned out to be future star Chris Tucker.

It was immediately clear to Foxx that he needed to get back to work and study his craft. He wanted to find a new edge in his comedy, understand his audience better, and perfect his delivery. Foxx was no longer on the top of his game, and he knew that, to succeed, he had to be the best. He decided on a new venture. First, he moved out of Los Angeles and into Las Vegas, Nevada, thinking that a change of scenery would be beneficial. Then, with the help of Warner Brothers, Foxx came up with a new idea for a television sitcom called *The Jamie Foxx Show.* For the next couple of years, Foxx worked with Warner Brothers to create and develop a show that would give him an opportunity for a new beginning and a chance to regain his comedic stature. It was both challenging and inspiring.

5

The Jamie Foxx Show

As he struggled to get back on top of his comedic game, Foxx finally got the break he had been waiting for since he moved from San Diego to Los Angeles: Fox Records signed him to record an album. In July 1994, Foxx released his debut album, *Peep This*, which comprised 13 tracks. On the R&B charts, *Peep This* reached number 12; it sold 300,000 copies. In addition, "Infatuation," a single from the album, was popular nationally. The overall success of Foxx's first music venture, however, was moderate and was quickly forgotten. Jamie Foxx had not reached music superstardom, and he was disappointed that the public regarded him more as a comedian than as a musician. He hoped to change that opinion one day.

Around the time that Foxx was filming his HBO special *Jamie Foxx: Straight From the Foxxhole*, he heard life-changing news: His ex-girlfriend informed him that he was going to become a father. Foxx was thrilled when his daughter, Corinne

Foxx's daughter, Corinne Marie, was born in 1995. Foxx has made a point of being involved in his daughter's life; he plans visits with her even when he's working on a movie far away from her home. Here, Foxx and Corinne are shown at the after-party for the premier of the movie *Atlantis: The Lost Empire*, in 2001. Corinne was six years old.

Marie, was born in 1995. He and his ex-girlfriend did not get back together, but they did decide to share the responsibilities of raising Corinne. Although Corinne lives with her mother, Foxx has been an active father figure who takes pleasure in spending time with his daughter. As she grows up, Foxx tries to be there to help with homework and do the types of things he missed with his own biological father. From the first moment he learned he was to become a father, Foxx felt an even greater, more urgent, reason to succeed: He wanted his daughter to be proud of him.

THE UPS AND DOWNS OF SHOWBIZ

Professionally, Foxx was looking forward to his new television venture. The sitcom that he had developed with Warner Brothers was ready to air. In 1996, *The Jamie Foxx Show* premiered on the WB network. Foxx was its co-creator (with Bentley Kyle Evans), star, and executive producer. The cast included Ellia English, Christopher B. Duncan, Garrett Morris (whom Foxx used to impersonate on *In Living Color*), and Garcelle Beauvais. The series became the WB's highest-rated series during its 1996–1997 season.

The Jamie Foxx Show ran for five years, from 1996 to 2001. Foxx played a struggling actor (also named Jamie) from Texas who tries to make it in Hollywood. Instead, his character ends up employed at a relatively unsuccessful hotel owned by his uncle (played by Garrett Morris). The sitcom gave Foxx time for other things, including spending time with and getting to know his young daughter, Corinne.

Foxx was reconnecting with his comedy and returning to the top. He had already spent five years in comedic roles, however, and he felt ready to take a break from comedy and try his hand at drama. It was difficult to get people to take him seriously. His widespread positive association with *In Living Color* had already firmly typecast him as a comedian, and it was going to be a hard stereotype to break. During his work with *The Jamie Foxx Show*, Foxx did fit in film projects, but they did not include dramas. In 1996, Foxx appeared as a minor character in *The Truth About Cats and Dogs*, a romantic comedy, and *The Great White Hype*, a boxing comedy.

Foxx's own television show, the eponymous *Jamie Foxx Show*, premiered in 1996 on the WB network. It was the network's top-rated show in the 1996–1997 season, and ran until 2001. This still from an episode shows Foxx with Ellia English, who played the aunt of Jamie King, Foxx's character.

Michael Lehmann directed *The Truth About Cats and Dogs*, starring Uma Thurman, Janeane Garofalo, and Ben Chaplin. Lehmann's previous films had included *Meet the Applegates* (1991) and *Airheads* (1994). Foxx played a character named Ed. The film, released in April, received positive reviews that called it delightful, lighthearted fun. *The Great White Hype*, directed by Reginald Hudlin, on the other hand, received lesser reviews. Hudlin had previously directed *House Party* (1990) and *Boomerang* (1992). *The Great White Hype* opened in May and boasted big-name actors like Samuel L. Jackson,

Jeff Goldblum, and Peter Berg; despite the famous actors, it was a box-office flop. Again, Foxx had a very small part in the film as Hassan El Ruk'n. His fellow *In Living Color* cast member Damon Wayans was also in the film. In addition to his small role, Foxx also wrote and performed a song for *The Great White Hype*, called "Knocked Nekked (From the Waist Down)." Foxx found the movie to be embarrassing: He knew it never came together and just was not funny.

Foxx was able to fit in another music project when he wrote and performed a song called "Experiment" for the family comedy film *Home Alone 3* in 1997. When Foxx still could not get a role in a dramatic movie, he continued to sign contracts for comedies. He appeared in three comedies in three consecutive years: *Booty Call*, *The Players Club*, and *Held Up*; all were poorly reviewed.

Jeff Pollack's *Booty Call* appeared in theaters in February 1997. Pollack had previously directed *Above the Rim* in 1994. In *Booty Call*, Foxx played Bunz, a lead character in this raunchy comedy. Also starring in the movie were Tommy

DID YOU KNOW?

Foxx thought he finally had his chance to land a dramatic role when he went to audition for writer/director Cameron Crowe's *Jerry Maguire* (1996), a movie that was to star Tom Cruise. Unfortunately, Foxx came across as too loud and brash during his reading for the role of Rod Tidwell, an egomaniacal football player. Actor Cuba Gooding Jr. got the role instead; Gooding then went on to win an Oscar from the Academy Awards for his performance in the film.

Although he failed the audition, Foxx did not let it get him down. He was still happy to have finally had the opportunity to audition for a drama, and he used it as a learning experience. He had been young and star struck, which showed during his audition, but when the camera was off, Foxx was more relaxed and he found that he got along well with Tom Cruise. They would later become friends.

Davidson, Vivica Fox, and Tamala Jones. Most movie critics had nothing positive to say about the movie or Foxx's role in it. *USA Today* wrote, "Anyone seeking a good time that involves wit and logic will consider [Booty Call] a definite wrong number." Comedian and television star Bill Cosby said he thought *Booty Call* was so crude that it should not have been made. Foxx understood Cosby's reaction to the movie, and he agreed with Cosby's main point that one should strive to do better things. Yet Foxx also felt that, at that time, he did not have many film options. Foxx took most of the roles he was offered, even if their quality dipped below what Foxx would have preferred, hoping that one day soon he would be offered better movies.

In April 1998, Foxx appeared in another comedy, *The Players Club*, written and directed by actor and hip-hop star Ice Cube. In addition to writing and directing the movie, Ice Cube also acted in it, along with Bernie Mac, Monica Calhoun, John Amos, and others. Reviewers did not care for the movie overall, but some spoke well of Foxx's contribution to the film. The *Film Journal International* wrote, "Comedians Bernie Mac, Jamie Foxx and A.J. Johnson . . . bring considerable snap and spark to their roles." Even better, the *San Francisco Chronicle* wrote, "Jamie Foxx adds easygoing charm as the club's disc jockey, who hates his life among the rats."

The third movie in Foxx's comedy run from 1997 to 1999 was *Held Up,* which hit the theaters in October 1999 and then quickly left. Film critics highly criticized this box-office flop directed by Steve Rash, who in 1978 had directed an award-winning film, *The Buddy Holly Story*. Critics called Foxx's performance as Michael Dawson "a misstep," saying that Foxx seemed tired and defeated and was uninteresting to watch. Other actors in the film included Nia Long, Barry Corbin, John Cullum, and Jake Busey.

Throughout these films, Foxx was still hard at work on his WB sitcom, *The Jamie Foxx Show*. In 1998, Foxx won a National

Association for the Advancement of Colored People (NAACP) Image Award for Outstanding Lead Actor in a Comedy Series for his efforts on the show. It felt good to be recognized by the important organization, which celebrates the outstanding achievements and performances of people of color in the arts. NAACP Image Awards include 36 competitive categories that cover motion pictures, television, music, and literature.

For the most part, Foxx felt that his career was pointing in the right direction. He continued to perform live stand-up comedy, and he was establishing himself in both television and film. Foxx felt indebted to the Bay Area Black Comedy Competition and Festival, which had been a big catalyst in helping him start his career back in 1991. In return, he wanted to help other unknown comedians of color.

As a result, Foxx coproduced a television project called *Jamie Foxx Presents Laffapalooza!* for Showtime (it would later change networks to Comedy Central) in 1998. The show, taped at the annual October Urban International Comedy Arts Festival in Atlanta, Georgia, served to help up-and-coming comedians get a start with their careers. The show has become a huge success, and today the festival spans a period of four days. Foxx is energetic and sassy as host, and the comedians are known to be explicit and streetwise. Through this project, Foxx helps give edgy, urban comedians—both known and unknown (such as Deon Cole, LaVell Crawford, and Rob Stapleton)—a venue in which to showcase their talent.

Foxx sees the Urban International Comedy Arts Festival as a great learning ground for comedians. He told an interviewer,

> What I love about *Laffapalooza!* [is that] it comes to Atlanta every fall, and it really gives people an opportunity to not only see me and some of my friends perform, but it also gives new talent a chance to get out there and showcase for the non-comics. . . . People really get an opportunity to see the new talent before they get their television and movie

deals. . . . People will begin to understand that this game of comedy is a challenge, but it is a chance for people to . . . have a lot of fun!

As someone who had his own share of struggles, Foxx knows how important it is to help black entertainers break into the entertainment business.

PERSISTENCE PAYS OFF

After years of trying to get a dramatic role in a movie, but finding little opportunity or failing auditions, Foxx's patience and persistence paid off in 1999 when he landed a small role in an Oliver Stone movie. *Any Given Sunday* opened in theaters in December. Stone, a prolific and respected director, had previously won two Oscars for Best Director: *Platoon* (1987) and *Born on the Fourth of July* (1990).

Actors Al Pacino (as head coach Tony D'Amata), Cameron Diaz (as Christina Pagniacci), Dennis Quaid (as Jack "Cap" Rooney), James Woods (as Dr. Harvey Mandrake), and LL Cool J (as "J Man") all contributed to the all-star cast of *Any Given Sunday*. Foxx gave one interviewer his take on *Any Given Sunday*: "It's about life, basically. Football just happens to be where we're playing it. Within life everybody has to struggle. Everybody is on top sometimes and then, the next thing you know, they're on the bottom."

It had not been easy for Foxx to secure his role as Willie Beamen, a second-string quarterback with a big ego. When director Stone first met Jamie Foxx, he was not impressed. Stone thought Foxx came across as a comic rather than as an actor. Then Stone asked him if he knew how to throw a football. To show Stone what he could do, Foxx put on his Deion Sanders number 21 Cowboys jersey and his Cowboys helmet; then he filmed his own mini-movie with a group of friends, in which he sang and played football. He even came up with a rap for Willie to perform. Stone liked the mini-movie, as well

Foxx's breakout role came when he was cast in Oliver Stone's *Any Given Sunday*, a drama about the inner workings of a professional football team. Although Stone was not initially impressed with Foxx, his mind changed when he saw what Foxx could do with a football.

as Foxx's charisma, and he gave Foxx the part. The rap Foxx had included on the audition tape even appeared in the movie during a montage sequence. Foxx also sang the theme song and outro (closing song), both entitled "Any Given Sunday," for the movie.

While making the movie, Foxx carefully observed Stone's directorial techniques. Working for the first time on a big-budget film, Foxx was surprised to have four, five, or six cameras filming at the same time. Previously, he had worked only with one-camera shots, where all actors had to stay within view. The larger scale of this production impressed Foxx. Stone, always busy on the set, encouraged a creative energy that stretched out to those around him. Producer Clayton

Townsend said, "Oliver sets goals for himself every day which seem to be impossible and he strives to keep pushing, to get that extra something. I've always noticed that when things seem to be peaceful and calm, he creates some commotion, which results in a highly creative three- or six-ring circus."

People often consider *Any Given Sunday* to be the breakout film that truly got Jamie Foxx's name into circulation, in both the eyes of moviegoers and moviemakers. Even though Foxx had broken his comedic typecast at last and proved that he had more depth as an actor, the film itself received mixed reviews. Critics found bits of the film entertaining, but they thought it was a disappointment as a whole. Of Jamie Foxx's role in the film, Roger Ebert said, "In a broken-field role that requires [Jamie Foxx] to be unsure and vulnerable, then cocky and insufferable, then political, then repentant, Foxx doesn't step wrong."

As a result of Foxx's success in *Any Given Sunday*, new doors began to open for him. People had seen that Foxx could, in fact, be a dramatic actor and had more to offer than comedic characters. Unfortunately, Foxx had yet to find a movie of compelling quality.

In September 2000, *Bait* appeared in theaters, starring Jamie Foxx as Alvin Sanders, an ex-con who the police use to catch

IN HIS OWN WORDS...

Foxx's first experience working on the big-budget film *Any Given Sunday* was an eye-opener. He had great respect and appreciation for what Oliver Stone was able to convey through the movie. Foxx explained to one interviewer what he expected audiences to get from *Any Given Sunday* in this way: "Even if you never played football, you can relate to somebody who's willing to die for something. You may not necessarily want to play football after watching this movie, because it's real crazy, but you might want to go after a dream with the same conviction that players bring to the game. That's the heart of the movie, man. Whatever it takes."

a killer. Antoine Fuqua, who directed *The Replacement Killers* in 1998, also directed the action thriller. *Bait* was not well received by critics, although many thought Foxx's acting was a bright spot in the contrived plot. The *San Francisco Chronicle* wrote, "two things pretty much save [*Bait*]. The last 40 minutes are well plotted and paced. And Foxx is enormously likable. As Alvin, [Jamie Foxx] is all bluster—a nervous wreck who talks a good game but is afraid of his own shadow. Then Foxx lets us see him come out from that shadow. It's a nice piece of comic acting."

On the set of *The Jamie Foxx Show*, Foxx continued his starring role. Despite its commercial success for the WB network, however, Foxx was never satisfied with the show; he considered it to be mediocre, and he knew in his heart that that was not enough. Foxx wanted the show to be special, but he felt it missed the mark. The final episode aired in 2001. In addition to the Image Award Foxx had won in 2000, he had been nominated for six others, including the Kids' Choice Awards for Favorite Television Actor in 2000 and 2001. Foxx, who always wants to have many projects in the works at once, continued to focus on what was to come.

A MAN OF MANY TALENTS

Foxx was not afraid to leave *The Jamie Foxx Show* behind; he saw the change as an opportunity to keep things fresh and new, as well as to make more time to do higher-caliber projects. In September 2001, he brought his new attitude to his role as host of the MTV Video Music Awards at New York's Metropolitan Opera House. Performers at the show included 'NSync (with Michael Jackson), Alicia Keys, Jennifer Lopez (with Ja Rule), Jay-Z, and U2.

Then, just three days after the MTV Video Music Awards, on September 11, 2001, the world changed forever. Terrorists, under orders from Osama bin Laden, attacked the World Trade Center in New York City and the Pentagon in Washington, D.C.

The terrorists had hijacked four commercial U.S. airplanes. They crashed the first plane into the north tower of the World Trade Center, and then crashed a second plane into the south tower. A third plane hit the Pentagon, and the fourth plane went down in a Pennsylvania field after some of the passengers tried to stop the hijackers. The people aboard all four planes were killed instantly. More than 3,000 people died because of the destruction the airplanes caused. Businesses crumbled. People lost their jobs and their homes. The cost to clean up the disasters totaled $600 million. The events of 9/11 would affect the lives of the American people for years to come.

People across the United States and around the world were stunned and horrified by the terrorist attacks. Foxx knew that he could not take life for granted, and he would continue to treasure the time he spent with Corinne, who was then six years old. Jolted by the 9/11 tragedies, Foxx strove to appreciate each day with a genuine passion and zest for life. Now, more than ever, he wanted to take his career to a new level.

Meanwhile, director Michael Mann (who had recently directed *Heat* in 1995 and *The Insider* in 1999) was working hard to bring to the screen a movie called *Ali* about heavyweight boxer Muhammad Ali. In order to make the film as authentic as possible, Mann worked extensively with actor Will Smith, who played the title role, for nearly two years before the film hit theaters in December 2001. Smith trained with former boxer and trainer Darrell Foster for months. Mann and Smith had to juggle a desire to be authentic with the limitations of a two-hour movie and the difficulties of portraying a living figure. They decided that Smith would try to capture an interpretation of Ali, rather than just impersonate him.

Foxx was cast as Ali's corner man, Drew "Bundini" Brown, a small role in the film. This was the first time Foxx would play a real person instead of a fictional character. He had done impressions of people before, but he had never had to portray them in film. As Brown, Foxx sought to play the role in a way that would cause audience members to forget it was Jamie Foxx and, instead, see only Brown. Lola Ogunnaike of the *New York Times* noted, "[Jamie Foxx's] portrayal of . . . Bundini Brown . . . solidified Mr. Foxx's status as an actor to watch. For that performance, he ballooned from 185 to 220 pounds and mastered Mr. Brown's underbite and peculiar speech patterns."

Although his part was small, Foxx received rave reviews for his performance in *Ali*. He won a Best Supporting Actor Black Reel Award and an Outstanding Supporting Actor in a Motion Picture NAACP Image Award. Roger Ebert said, "Jamie Foxx is...engaging and appealing as Bundini, the self-destructive mascot who sold the champs belt 'and put it into my arm.'" The *Houston Chronicle* called Jamie Foxx "impressive," and the *Village Voice* called him "outstanding." Will Smith's extensive research and hours of training paid off, as well. Smith was nominated for an Oscar for Best Actor. At last, Foxx had found himself in a winning movie—at the box office, with critics, and with fans.

Between his hectic movie schedules, Foxx returned to comedy in February 2002, when HBO Television produced Foxx's second stand-up comedy show, entitled *Jamie Foxx: I Might Need Security*. Foxx performed his stand-up routine to a sold-out crowd at the Paramount Theater in Oakland, California. The HBO show was available on DVD by June of the same year.

Just one year later, Foxx came out with his third comedy show on DVD, this one called *Jamie Foxx Unleashed: Lost, Stolen and Leaked!* Although the DVD appeared in stores in 2003, the actual tour from which it was taken was performed in 1997. In this physical comedy, Foxx uses his entire body as he works the full length of the stage in his hometown state, Texas. Foxx engages the audience with impersonations, talking about women and dating, and discussing angry rap lyrics. In an extra feature on the DVD, Foxx and his half sister, Deidra Dixon, perform a duet on the piano.

In 2003, Foxx teamed up with established rappers Twista and Kanye West to record the song "Slow Jamz," little knowing what a huge hit it would become. In addition to his growing fame as an actor, Foxx's talents as a musician were beginning to be recognized. Here, Foxx performs with Kanye West (right) during the fortieth anniversary party for *Rolling Stone* magazine.

On the movie front, Foxx was working on his role of Larry Jennings in the movie *Shade*. In his directorial debut, Damian Nieman gives viewers a look into the lives of poker hustlers working the clubs in Los Angeles, California. *Shade* premiered in June 2003. Other actors in the movie included Stuart Townsend, Gabriel Byrne, Thandie Newton, Melanie Griffith, and Sylvester Stallone. Once again, Foxx had landed himself a role in a film that critics, for the most part, praised.

Despite a few disappointments in 2003, Foxx ended the year on a high note with a musical success. He teamed up with Kanye West and Twista to record "Slow Jamz." The song appeared first in January 2004 on Twista's album *Kamikaze*, where it rose, due in part to the success of the hit single "Slow

Kanye West and Hip-Hop

Kanye West was born on June 8, 1977. His father was a former Black Panther (an African-American political group that promoted civil rights), and his mother was a college professor. West's parents divorced when he was three, and West and his mother settled in Chicago. Inspired by Run-D.M.C. and with aspirations to become a rapper, West quickly fell in love with hip-hop (a popular urban youth culture) and found he had a talent for beat making, even creating a signature beat-making style. Before he made a name for himself as an artist, West established a reputation as a producer, working on producing albums for artists like Jay-Z, Janet Jackson, and Eminem.

Since then, West has become highly successful with the release of three albums, all by Roc-A-Fella/Def Jam: *The College Dropout* (2004), *Late Registration* (2005), and *Graduation* (2007). *The College Dropout* and *Late Registration* received a combined total of six Grammy Awards; *Graduation* received three. Critics have called the outspoken and confident West the most important creative force in hip-hop music today. West has a unique sound that has caught on quickly in the music industry.

In the 1990s, artistic visionary Russell Simmons began thinking about how to solve problems in his community. Simmons hoped to bring about social changes for black inner-city youth by rapping about street life. Simmons first co-created a record label called Def Jam in 1984; that label would become a parent label to Roc-A-Fella in 2004. Simmons helped start the careers of rappers Run-D.M.C., Public Enemy, LL Cool J, the Beastie Boys, and Will Smith.

The HBO television series *Def Comedy Jam* ran from 1992 to 1997. Critics call the Def Jam comedians "raw" and "outrageous." Martin Lawrence was the first host. Jamie Foxx appeared on the show, and his appearance (along with Martin Lawrence, Chris Tucker, and others) was later put onto a DVD called *Def Comedy Jam: All Stars 5*, in 2001. *Def Comedy Jam* predominately allowed a place for African Americans to showcase their work—Dave Chappelle, D.L. Hughley, Bernie Mac, and Chris Rock, to name just a few.

Jamz," to number 1 on the charts. Then, one month later, West included a longer version of the song on his debut album, *College Dropout*. This version of "Slow Jamz" included an intro and two extra verses by Jamie Foxx, and it excludes the original outro by Twista. "Slow Jamz" was a popular song played on mainstream radio, and all three collaborating artists received high praises for their work on the song.

6

Reaching Stardom

The year was 2004 and, looking back, Jamie Foxx might consider his smash-hit single, "Slow Jamz," the perfect start to what would prove to be a nearly perfect year for him. In the coming months, Foxx's career would reach new heights. Although he would not reach his goal of superstar status as a musician, he would be well on his way to being a Hollywood superstar.

In February 2004, Foxx headed to the Beverly Hills Hotel to attend Clive Davis's pre-Grammy party. Davis's parties were the place to be, and only the best of the best were invited. Davis had been a leader in the music industry since 1967, when he became president of CBS Records. When he worked with CBS, Davis was credited with discovering famed artists like Janis Joplin, Bruce Springsteen, Billy Joel, and Santana. When Davis founded Arista Records, he signed future stars like Patti Smith, Sarah McLachlan, Whitney Houston, and Sean "Diddy" Combs. In 2000, when Davis founded J Records, he signed new

Excited by the success of "Slow Jamz," Foxx wanted to pursue his musical career further, and he thought his best chance was with longtime industry insider Clive Davis. He won Davis over with a surprise performance at Davis's 2004 pre-Grammy party. Here, Foxx is shown with Davis at the 2006 pre-Grammy party.

stars, like Alicia Keys, as well as established artists such as Rod Stewart and Luther Vandross. Jamie Foxx hoped to be Clive Davis's next big discovery.

Foxx wanted a chance to win Davis over with his singing abilities, but it was difficult to set up an appointment. He decided to try another approach. He went to the Grammy party with friends Kanye West and Twista, who were to perform at the party. Although Foxx was not scheduled to perform, he introduced West and Twista to the crowd and then stayed, sneaking in a performance of the current hit single "Slow

Jamz" with West and Twista. Later in the evening, Foxx joined Alicia Keys and Angie Stone in a song, much to the delight of the guests. Foxx's plan to win over Clive Davis worked. By the end of the evening, Davis offered Foxx an album deal with J Records. Davis recognized Foxx's natural passion for music, and he was ready to help him create an album that expressed that passion.

THE STAN "TOOKIE" WILLIAMS STORY

During 2004, Foxx starred in four movies, three of which were well received: *Redemption: The Stan Tookie Williams Story* (for television), *Breakin' All the Rules* (the one film that critics did not like), *Collateral*, and *Ray*. Foxx received numerous nominations and awards for his movies, and the public started to see that Foxx was a competent actor who could thoroughly transform himself into character. He was not just a comedian, a songwriter, a singer, and a musician; he was also a serious actor.

Redemption: The Stan Tookie Williams Story, a movie made for television, aired on FX in March 2004. This project meant a lot to Foxx. Once again, it was about a real person. At the time, Williams was still living and had a story to tell. People were talking about Tookie's story across the country. Tookie was one of the founding members of the Crips, a Los Angeles street gang. In 1979, Tookie was sentenced to death for the murder of four people on two separate occasions. Although Tookie admitted that he had a violent past, he maintained his innocence until the very end. Foxx, along with numerous other supporters, like Jesse Jackson, felt that Tookie had redeemed himself during his time in prison and should not be put to death.

Tookie did use his time on death row to better himself. While he was in solitary confinement, Tookie had begun to read, write, and draw to help him survive. Much of the material he wrote denounced gang violence. He also wrote children's books with anti-gang messages. The work he produced led to a nomination for the Nobel Peace Prize and the Nobel Prize in Literature. Yet, true to his sentence, on December 13, 2005, Stanley Tookie Williams was executed by lethal injection at the San Quentin State Penitentiary. It was also Jamie Foxx's thirty-eighth birthday. Foxx would later tell interviewer Chris Rolls,

> I wasn't there for the funeral . . . I actually spoke to Stanley the night that they executed him. It was the most incredible, most disappointing, most exciting, most crazy feeling I've ever experienced in my life. . . . But what I take from it is nothing but peace, which [is what Stanley] told me to take from it . . .[Stanley told Foxx] to keep on promoting [Stanley's] words for peaceful things.

Vondie Curtis-Hall, who had previously directed episodes of the popular television series *ER* and *Firefly*, among other things, directed *Redemption*. The film covers Tookie's life as he grew up in a rough neighborhood of Louisiana, got involved in street gangs in Los Angeles, and ended up on death row. Foxx starred as Tookie, bringing to life Tookie's struggles with redemption. The *San Diego Union-Tribune* wrote, "The presence of Jamie Foxx, heretofore known primarily as a comic, in the role of Williams makes 'Redemption' all the more interesting. But his frank, understated performance as Williams offers far more than novelty appeal. Easily worthy of an Emmy nomination, it establishes Foxx as a serious actor to reckon with." Foxx received recognition for his leading actor role in the film with a Black Reel Award, an NAACP Image Award, a Grace Award, and a Golden Satellite Award. Foxx was also nominated for a Golden Globe, an Independent Spirit Award, and a Screen Actors Guild (SAG) Award.

BREAKIN' ALL THE RULES

Working on *Redemption* had been a great experience for Foxx; he had really put his heart and soul into it. Once that was finished, he looked forward to the next project. He still enjoyed comedies, but he found it difficult to get roles in high-quality comic movies. Many of the comedy scripts that passed by his desk were not worth even looking at. At this time, Martin Lawrence, Chris Rock, and Chris Tucker, who were all black comedians of a similar age, were getting offered comedic roles in the larger movies. Foxx found that he had to grab nearly all of the opportunities that came his way, even those lacking in substance and artistic merit, in order to keep his name out there.

In one such romantic comedy, *Breakin' All the Rules,* which appeared in theaters in May, Foxx plays the leading man, Quincy Watson. Daniel Taplitz, who wrote and directed the film, had previously directed a number of television shows, and, most recently, a movie called *Commandments* (1997). Like many of Foxx's other comedies to date, *Breakin' All the Rules* had mostly negative reviews. Many critics felt that Foxx and his costar, Gabrielle Union, would have shone more brightly if they had better material. Some thought that Foxx's charisma and charm were enough to carry the movie, but others thought the writing and pacing were too poor to save the movie.

COLLATERAL

Foxx's next project, however, was a winner: It had good directing, a good script, and a good cast. In *Collateral,* Foxx was able to work with Michael Mann once again. In this movie, which appeared in theaters in August 2004, Foxx played a cabdriver named Max opposite Tom Cruise. It had been a long time since Foxx had auditioned for a role in *Jerry Maguire,* and he had done a lot of growing up since then. He and Cruise instantly hit it off and worked well together on-screen.

Under the direction of Mann, Foxx knew that there would be a lot of rehearsal. Foxx told interviewer George Roush, "With Michael Mann, you're going to rehearse so much until

Foxx's performance as cabdriver Max in 2004's *Collateral* won him much critical acclaim. Here, Foxx is shown in a scene from the movie along with Tom Cruise and Barry Shabaka Henley.

you're almost numb, but what happens is, is that now when you start, you're not acting at all, you're just that person." As the rehearsals got under way, Foxx did just that and he became Max.

Cruise plays a hit man, Vincent, who gets into Max's (Foxx's) cab. A relationship forms between Vincent and Max and becomes more complicated as the movie moves along. Usually, actors are able to make a connection with each other by looking at each other directly, but in this movie, many of Cruise and Foxx's scenes together took place in the cab, with both characters looking straight ahead. Foxx told interviewer Remy Crane, "The interesting and challenging thing about filming in a cab was that we did a great deal of our acting and interacting without looking into the eyes of my fellow actors. Rather, many of my lines were delivered when I was looking ahead and they were responding by talking to the back of my head." Consequently, they adjusted the cab's rearview mirror so that Foxx could look up and make a connection with Cruise in the mirror. This helped to pull off the intensity that the two characters were feeling in their scenes.

Foxx received enthusiastic reviews for his portrayal of Max. Roger Ebert said, "Jamie Foxx's work is a revelation. I've thought of [Jamie Foxx] in terms of comedy . . . but here he steps into a dramatic lead and is always convincing and involving." *Rolling Stone* said, "If all you know of Foxx is from TV sitcoms and movie drool (*Breakin' All the Rules*), you're in for a shock. This is Foxx's year. . . . Foxx fires up the screen with the power and subtlety of a born star. And his teamwork with Cruise is a thing of beauty." Foxx's work in *Collateral* brought him nominations for Best Supporting Actor with the Academy Awards, Golden Globes, SAG, and British Academy of Film and Television Arts (BAFTA). Foxx won a Black Reel Award for Best Supporting Actor for *Collateral*.

BECOMING RAY

Meanwhile, director Taylor Hackford was trying to cast the lead in his upcoming movie, a biographical film about the legendary blues singer and pianist Ray Charles. Hackford had

IN HIS OWN WORDS...

Foxx has worked on three films with director Michael Mann: *Ali* (2001), *Collateral* (2004), and *Miami Vice* (2006). The director and actor team has a good working relationship, and Foxx has said that he appreciates the way Mann approaches film. Foxx says of Mann: "When you're working with Michael Mann I don't think the first thing you think about is the commercial success. The first thing you think about is the art of it. When you look at Al Pacino and his body of work, most of the films, the ones you remember, weren't a commercial success."

previously directed numerous movies, including *White Nights* (1985), *Bound by Honor* (1993), *The Devil's Advocate* (1997), and, most recently, *Proof of Life* (2000).

It had taken Hackford a long time to get to the point where he was ready to choose his star actor for *Ray*. He and producer Stuart Benjamin had worked to get financing for the film for 15 years. Billionaire Philip Anschutz finally agreed to cofinance the movie with a studio, but unfortunately, Hackford and Benjamin could not find a studio to back the other half. Anschutz wanted the project under way, so he told Hackford he would finance the entire film. With full financing in place, Hackford could finally bring to life the movie he had wanted for so long.

Hackford had seen Foxx in *Any Given Sunday* and *Ali*, and he saw what a range of characters Foxx could play. He knew that Foxx had talent and a lot of potential. Foxx also had the right look, with a square jawline and lean body similar to that of Ray Charles. Then Hackford found out that Foxx could sing and that he had extensive training in classical piano. At that point, Hackford knew he had his lead actor. Actresses Kerry Washington and Regina King played the lead female roles in the film.

Once Hackford decided on Foxx, he worked to get Foxx the inspiration he needed. Hackford arranged for Foxx to meet with Ray Charles himself before filming began. They wanted Charles to approve of the actor who would represent him in the film. What would Ray Charles think of Jamie Foxx playing him? Hackford told Sean Daly of the *Washington Post*, "Believe me, [Ray Charles is] not easy. . . . If he wanted to stop this project at any moment, he could have."

Almost immediately after introductions, the two musicians sat down at the piano together and started to play songs between conversations. Charles would play a little funk or a little blues and Jamie would play it back. Then Charles wanted to hear Foxx play some jazz. Charles began to play music by Thelonious Monk (1917–1982) and then turned it over

Perhaps his greatest performance to date, Jamie Foxx's portrayal of Ray Charles in the biopic *Ray* won him great critical acclaim, plus an Oscar. Director Taylor Hackford set up a meeting between Charles and Foxx to make sure that Charles approved of the actor who would play him.

to Foxx. Thelonious Monk's music is difficult to play, and Foxx had never tried it before this meeting. Monk had such an original sound that even his most devoted followers have trouble imitating it.

Hackford told Daly, "Jamie's background wasn't jazz; all Ray cared about was jazz. So Jamie's not playing, and Ray's like, 'Come on, man! It's like this!' And Jamie's not getting it. And Ray shouts, 'Come on, man, it's right under your fingers.'" Foxx listened, kept at it, and did not give up. Hackford told Daly, "And then, finally, Jamie got it. He stood his ground. He wasn't humiliated. He stayed with it, and he got Thelonious Monk. And at that moment, Ray stood up and started hugging himself and said: 'That's it. The kid's got it. He's the one.' Jamie grew to about 10 feet tall. He was anointed by the master." Foxx knew that Charles believed in what he could do and, at that moment, Jamie Foxx believed it, too. The entire meeting lasted only a couple of hours, but Foxx was nonetheless honored to meet, share stories, and play the piano with the 73-year-old R&B superstar.

To understand what the young Ray Charles was like, Foxx studied old cassette tapes of the prime-time variety series *The Dinah Shore Show* (which aired from 1951 to 1956, and won the Emmy award twice) in which Shore speaks to Ray Charles. From the tapes, Foxx learned to mimic Charles's habits and mannerisms. Foxx also spoke to Charles's children and friends, including longtime friend Quincy Jones. Foxx attended classes at the Braille Institute and listened to endless blues, jazz, and soul music. Gradually, he started to put together Charles's background, personality, and talents into a character that he could embody.

In order to convincingly play the wiry Charles, Foxx lost more than thirty pounds, going from a brawny 190 pounds to 157. Foxx worked with his own fitness guru, Rashan Kahn, with whom Foxx had been training on and off since *Any Given Sunday*. Before he worked with Foxx, Kahn had been an assistant to Richard Pryor in the 1980s. To prepare Foxx to lose the necessary weight for his role in *Ray*, Kahn told Foxx that he could do anything if he set his mind to it. Kahn did not believe in putting restrictions on Foxx's diet, but he left it up to Foxx to find the willpower. He suggested that Foxx eat frequent, smaller meals; Kahn then instructed Foxx to work out between these small meals. The workouts ensured that Foxx would maintain his muscle, as well as lose pounds faster. In this way, Kahn reworked Foxx's metabolism.

Foxx also underwent long hours in the makeup room to get fitted for his prosthetics, which covered and glued his eyes shut. This caused Foxx to be "blind" during each day of filming. When Charles was seven, his right eye was removed, probably as a result of glaucoma, but doctors were not sure at the time.

For the film, Hackford ordered the prosthetics to be modeled after Charles's damaged eyelids. Foxx later told a reporter that he felt "closed up" when he first started wearing the prosthetics, with a sense of panic that nearly led to hyperventilation. It was difficult to do anything without his sight. Foxx had to depend on assistants to lead him on and off the set.

Foxx practiced the piano segments for the film for hours; he performed every piano piece himself. He also sang the

Ray Charles

Ray Charles was born on September 23, 1930, in Albany, Georgia. At age seven, he lost his sight to undiagnosed glaucoma (abnormally high fluid pressure in the eye, which can harden the eyeball and cause partial to complete loss of vision). Soon after, he attended the Florida School for the Deaf and Blind, located in St. Augustine. In school, Charles learned to play the piano; he read three or four bars of music printed in Braille at a time, memorized it, practiced it, repeated that procedure, and then played the whole piece altogether.

Charles's mother died when he was 15 years old, and he went to live with his mother's friends, a couple who lived in Jacksonville, Florida. From there, he started to get jobs playing gigs with various bands, eventually moving to Seattle, Washington. Finally, in 1951, Ray Charles released his own R&B record, called *Baby, Let Me Hold Your Hand*. For the next 50 years, Charles recorded albums in various genres, including swing, jazz, R&B, soul, pop, and gospel. His last album, *Genius Loves Company*, appeared in stores in August 2004, two months after his death. It won Grammy awards for both album and record of the year.

On June 10, 2004, Ray Charles died in Beverly Hills, California, at the age of 73. Although he did not live to attend *Ray* in theaters, Hackford had arranged for Charles to listen to a pre-edited version. Charles loved it and was pleased that the movie had been made. Before his death, Charles told an interviewer, "I can't believe how good [Foxx] is. I've had a couple of people who saw him work and they came back and said, 'Ray, you just won't believe this guy! He's got you down so pat that he even walks like you! He does everything exactly like you.' I only go by my personal experience with him and I think he's phenomenal. He's a wonderful man."

following songs in *Ray*: "Get Your Kicks on Route 66," "Straighten Up and Fly Right," "I Got a Woman," "Mary Ann," and "Hit the Road, Jack."

How would Ray Charles react to the film? Hackford and Foxx had put long hours into the project. Would their hard work and dedication pay off? Hackford put together a rough cut of the film for Charles to listen to a few months before *Ray* would open in theaters. Hackford told Daly of the *Washington Post*, "The first thing [Charles] wanted to hear was his mama's voice, who I [Hackford] had cast. Talk about pressure. He was like a stone. He just sat there, frown on his face, quiet, not moving. He listened to three scenes, and I'm thinking, 'This is a disaster.' And then he started going, 'That's right. That's the truth.' And finally he said, 'Taylor, I'm really pleased. I'm very happy.'"

In October, Foxx emceed a concert to honor Ray Charles, who had died from liver disease on June 10, 2004 at age 73. Charles had been ill for some time and had stayed out of the public eye for the final three months of his life. Other entertainers (either presenting or performing) who joined Foxx at the concert included Tom Cruise, Mary J. Blige, Morgan

DID YOU KNOW?

Jamie Foxx became the first person ever to be nominated for three Golden Globe acting awards and four Screen Actors Guild (SAG) awards in the same year.

Golden Globe nominations:

Ray (Best Actor, which he won; and Best Motion Picture in Musical or Comedy); *Collateral* (Best Supporting Actor); *Redemption: The Stan Tookie Williams Story* (Best Actor in a Miniseries or a Motion Picture Made for Television)

SAG nominations:

Ray (Best Leading Actor, which he won; and Best Performance by a Cast in a Motion Picture); *Collateral* (Best Supporting Actor); *Redemption: The Stan Tookie Williams Story* (Best Actor in a Television Movie or Miniseries)

Freeman, Elton John, and Stevie Wonder. The concert, *Genius: A Night for Ray Charles*, was taped at Staples Center in Los Angeles, California, and aired on CBS television just a week before *Ray* opened in theaters in October.

The response from critics to the movie *Ray* was overwhelmingly positive, and Foxx himself received rave reviews. Critics called Jamie Foxx immensely talented, brilliant, and mesmerizing. Foxx's ability to capture the nuances of what made Ray Charles who he was—how he spoke to his children, answered the phone, got angry, and got happy—proved that Foxx was a gifted and credible actor.

A PAINFUL GOOD-BYE

Just before *Ray* appeared in theaters across the country, Jamie Foxx would have to say goodbye to one of the most important people in his life. His grandmother, Estelle Marie Talley, died in October 2004 at the age of 85. She had suffered from Alzheimer's for the last 10 years of her life. Estelle had been Foxx's greatest supporter, and her death deeply saddened him. She had made sacrifices to ensure that he had his piano lessons; she had arranged gigs to expose Foxx to work in the real world; she had enforced discipline and order at all times in her household to instill in Foxx the value of respect; and she had given her heart to the seven-month-old baby she had adopted all those years before. Estelle had understood him more than anyone else had. She knew his fears, as well as his hopes and dreams.

Foxx returned to his hometown of Terrell to attend Estelle's funeral. He was too emotional to read the eulogy, but Foxx's good friend Gilbert Willie agreed to do it for him. One of the hardest things Foxx had ever done was to say good-bye to the woman who had acted as his mother and who had been such a driving force in his life.

Foxx wanted to show his thanks and appreciation to his adoptive mother. Then Foxx was offered the opportunity to host the sixth annual CBS special, *A Home for the Holidays*, a one-hour television show. The Dave Thomas Foundation for Adoption and Children's Action Network presented the special. Foxx was happy to take part in the program and welcomed the chance to pay tribute to his grandmother.

A Home for the Holidays spotlighted stories of adoption, interspersed with musical performances. Rod Stewart sang "What a Wonderful World," as well as a duet with Jamie Foxx; Kenny G and Chaka Khan sang a duet, "Beautiful"; the Black-Eyed Peas sang "Where Is the Love?" and "Let's Get It Started"; Train sang "Calling All Angels"; Ashlee Simpson sang "Pieces of Me"; and Jamie Foxx sang "Heaven." In addition to the performers, actors Bruce Willis, Rene Russo, Dennis Quaid, and Jamie Lee Curtis all joined the show to introduce real adoption stories, which helped to raise awareness. It also gave Foxx a forum in which to share his admiration for and gratitude to Estelle, his biological grandmother and his adoptive mother.

7

Rolling Out
the Red Carpet

After an extraordinary year in 2004, audiences wondered what Foxx would do next. He had already proved himself in stand-up comedy, in film, and in music. In addition to being a distinguished actor, he had gained a reputation for being smart and funny. Foxx continued to live life to its fullest, working hard and partying hard. Although Foxx would reach new heights with his fame and fortune, he also remained focused and kept working on improving his multitude of talents.

On February 13, 2005, Foxx appeared at the Staples Center in Los Angeles for the 47th Annual Grammy Awards, hosted by Queen Latifah. Also at the show was Foxx's good friend Kanye West, who had won a Grammy for his collaboration with Alicia Keys for Best R&B Song, "You Don't Know My Name." West also took home Grammy awards for Best Rap Song for his hit "Jesus Walks," and Best Rap Album for *The College Dropout*.

At the 2005 Grammy Awards, Jamie Foxx and Alicia Keys (right) performed "Georgia on my Mind" as a tribute to the late Ray Charles.

Foxx performed at the awards show. As a tribute to Ray Charles, he sang "Georgia on My Mind" as a duet with Alicia Keys; Quincy Jones conducted the orchestra that backed them up. Before he launched into the song, Foxx murmured into the microphone, "For an old friend." Then Foxx (wearing a black tuxedo with a white shirt and a white tie, playing at a black piano) and Keys (wearing all white and playing at a white piano) gave an emotional, heartfelt performance.

THE 77TH ANNUAL ACADEMY AWARDS

The 77th Annual Academy Awards fell on Sunday, February 27, 2005. A few days before the show, Oprah Winfrey presented *Oprah's Oscar Extravaganza*, in which six actors interviewed each other; the interviews were aired on Oprah's prime-time television special. The actors who were paired to interview each other were George Clooney and Julia Roberts, Nicole Kidman and Russell Crowe, and Jamie Foxx and

Sidney Poitier (who won an Oscar for his leading role in *Lilies of the Field*, 1963).

In his interview, Foxx asked Poitier, who has six daughters, if he had any advice on fatherhood. Poitier responded, "You say what you feel you must say. As long as it's protective, she'll know that. And as long as it is in her best interest, she'd know that as well. Just talk it through. Always talk it through." With a preteen daughter of his own, Fox could well appreciate Poitier's words.

When Poitier asked Foxx if he saw marriage in his future, Foxx replied that he did not. He explained that, before he married, he would want to lose all of his fame, because, "If I didn't have what I have right now—all of the success—it may make it easier to find that person that really just wants you for you."

Fellow comedian Chris Rock hosted the 77th Annual Academy Awards live show. Some 42.1 million people tuned in to watch the show on television. It was a big night for Foxx, who was nominated for two awards: Best Supporting Actor for his work in *Collateral* and Best Actor for his work in *Ray*. Foxx went home with the Best Actor award, the third black actor in the history of the Academy Awards to do so. Sidney Poitier had become the first black actor to win the Best Actor award in 1964. Denzel Washington was the second black man to win the Best Actor award in 2001 for his role in *Training Day*. (Also in 2001, Halle Berry was the first black woman to win the Oscar for Best Actress.)

In addition to the Oscar for his performance in *Ray*, Jamie Foxx earned a host of other awards, including the NAACP Image Award, Black Entertainment Television (BET) Award, Golden Globe, and the SAG Award. The critics all seemed to agree that Jamie Foxx had done his best work for his interpretation of Ray Charles.

The Oscar changed Foxx's life in ways he did not expect. He pushed himself even harder to stay focused and to get the high-caliber roles he wanted. Although photographers constantly snapped pictures, reporters shouted out questions, and fans wanted his autograph, he would not let himself get distracted. Foxx told an interviewer with www.reel.com,

> You cannot look at things like the Oscars and other awards like a competition, you just have to allow them to happen. When you do your craft and you do your art, you do it simply for what it is. You want to be able to touch somebody in a certain way. . . . You just have to focus on doing great things with great people, based on great material. And whatever else happens, happens.

Foxx also knew that as a black actor he had to remember what his grandmother had taught him: He must always work harder and give more. He intended to do just that.

In his personal life, Foxx enjoyed his relationship with his daughter, Corinne, who still lived with her mother. Foxx was able to do things with his daughter that his biological parents had not taken the time and interest to do with him. It is important to Foxx to feel that he is a part of his daughter's life and to know that he has a meaningful role in her upbringing. He told Honie Stevens with *Ventana* magazine, "I want to be a man who shows up for her . . . I want to have such a big influence on her so that she knows she can call on me for anything— which she does." Despite the fact that Corinne has a celebrity father, the two still share quiet movie nights together now and then. Foxx also tries to attend her school functions and sporting events whenever his schedule allows. Although his busy Hollywood calendar keeps Foxx from being with Corinne in person on a daily basis, the father and daughter are frequently to video chat.

highly sought-after bachelor, Foxx is often in the com-
omen. With his good looks, dapper style, charm,
knows how to be the "southern gentleman" his
had taught him to be. During his involvement

with *Ray*, Foxx was dating actress/model Leila Arcieri, the former Miss San Francisco. Foxx has dated numerous women, and although he occasionally has relationships that last a while, he has not yet chosen to make a commitment to any one woman.

GOLD DIGGER

Kanye West invited Foxx to join him once again as a guest singer for a song called, "Gold Digger." The song, released by Roc-A-Fella/Def Jam in August, became a worldwide smash hit and held the number 1 spot on the Billboard Hot 100 for 10 consecutive weeks in 2005. The single also broke a record for the most digital downloads in a single week, reaching 80,000. (Since then, however, that record has been broken.) "Gold Digger" was included on Kanye West's newest album, *Late Registration*.

One year later, the friends teamed up to sing the popular song for the 48th Annual Grammy Awards on February 8, 2006, back at the Staples Center in Los Angeles. West won Grammy awards for: Best Rap Solo Performance for his rap portion on the song "Gold Digger," Best Rap Song for "Diamonds From Sierra Leone," and Best Rap Album for *Late Registration*.

DISASTER STRIKES

After *Late Registration*, the album with the hit single "Gold Digger," appeared in stores, disaster struck the southern United States. On August 25, 2005, Hurricane Katrina hit just north of Miami, Florida. Four days later, the eye of the hurricane hit Louisiana early in the morning. Much of the levee system in New Orleans collapsed a few hours later, which caused Lake Pontchartrain and the Mississippi River to flood nearly all of New Orleans. The hurricane damaged coastal regions of Mississippi and Alabama, as well as Louisiana. More than 1,000 people died as a result of the hurricane. Katrina caused approximately $200 billion in damage, and it displaced more than one million people. Thousands of displaced people were bused to neighboring states, including Texas, Foxx's home state.

When Hurricane Katrina destroyed parts of Louisiana, Mississippi, and Alabama, Foxx wanted to help. As a spokesperson for the NAACP's disaster relief fund for Hurricane Katrina, Foxx flew to Houston's Astrodome to serve food to hungry refugees at the camp there for people who had to move because of the hurricane. He also visited Dallas, Texas, to talk to the displaced people there and give them hope and encouragement. Although the whole experience greatly saddened him, he found some bright spots. Foxx drew inspiration from his conversations with the numerous preachers involved in the effort, and he valued the time he spent listening to the heart-wrenching stories of survivors, some of which brought him hope and encouragement. Foxx also traveled to Miami Beach, Florida, where he teamed up with Colin Farrell and other celebrities to raise money for Hurricane Katrina victims.

During the aftermath of the hurricane, Foxx's good friend Kanye West was featured on an NBC hurricane relief fundraiser. During his screen time, West asserted that President George W. Bush did not care about black people. Some Americans felt his remarks had gone too far, but Foxx stood by his friend. In an interview with entertainment journalist Kam Williams, Foxx said,

> Whatever [Kanye West] said, I stand by him. He made a good point. Think about what the Presidency used to stand for. When we were coming up as kids, it looked like the most heralded job, and you had to be the smartest, and like a father, where the United States is your family. Now it's almost a joke. If I was president, and my family was going through a crisis, I would have to go down there and check on my family.

appeared in two more movies: *Stealth* and *Jar-*, directed by Rob Cohen, was released in July. In this action drama, Foxx costarred with Josh Lucas and Jessica Biel. *Stealth* got terrible reviews, with some calling it loud and predictable. The three actors played stealth bomber pilots who worked to straighten out an artificial intelligence program. Roger Ebert said, "[*Stealth*] might be of interest to you if you want to see lots of jet airplanes going real fast and making a lot of noise, and if you don't care that the story doesn't merely defy logic, but strips logic bare, cremates it and scatters its ashes."

In *Jarhead*, Jamie was flattered and intrigued to have the opportunity to work with Oscar-winning British director Sam Mendes. Mendes had previously directed *Cabaret* (1993), *Company* (1996), *American Beauty* (1999), and *Road to Perdition* (2002). Mendes had won an Oscar and a Golden Globe for Best Director for his work on *American Beauty*.

Jarhead was based on a memoir by the same name written by Anthony Swofford. The book followed Swofford's time as a marine during the Persian Gulf War in 1991, when he was 20 years old. William Broyles Jr. (another ex-marine and an Academy Award nominee for *Apollo 13*) turned the book into a screenplay. Although Foxx would have a supporting role in the movie, he wanted the chance to work with Mendes and to be a part of the film, which he felt was a good story with a lot to tell. Also in the movie were Jake Gyllenhaal (playing Anthony Swofford), Scott MacDonald, and Peter Sarsgaard.

Foxx enjoyed his work on the set and found it refreshing to work with Mendes, who had a way of keeping the atmosphere on the set light, which helped when making a film like this. As in the book, the movie *Jarhead* follows former marine Anthony Swofford's pre-Desert Storm experiences in Saudi Arabia, as well as his time fighting in Kuwait. Foxx, who played Sergeant Sykes, had just finished filming *Stealth*, so he was familiar with playing a military character.

Jarhead, a movie about the First Gulf War, appeared in theaters in November 2005 at the time the Second Gulf War (also known as the Iraq War) was currently being foug

The Second Gulf War had started on March 20, 2003, when the United States invaded Iraq on the suspicion that Iraq possessed weapons of mass destruction. Some movie critics pointed out that the American public learned so much about the current Gulf War on their nightly television news that many were not going to be willing to see a movie about the First Gulf War. Overall, movie critics praised the cinematography and the performances by the actors, but they thought *Jarhead* did not quite make an emotional connection with the audience.

Author Anthony Swofford had a different reaction to the movie, which he saw as a piece of art that authentically captured the feelings of what it was like to be a part of a war. As he told an interviewer,

> After a few scenes I got used to an actor on screen being called Swofford. I recognized the story of *Jarhead* being told, the intense narrative tale and the more subtle and nuanced psychological and metaphysical storytelling strands that punctuate and intensify the war experience for Swoff[ord] and his cohorts. War in the real world is about winning, but war in art is about the expansion of feeling and the explosion of emotion, meaning and beauty.

Swofford had not originally written his memoirs to create an antiwar message, nor did he think the movie did, either. Both the book and the movie seemed to Swofford to be truthful depictions of the ugly realities of war.

UNPREDICTABLE

x's smooth R&B album, *Unpredictable*, was released in
her 2005. When one interviewer asked him about the
etween albums (it had been 12 years since *Peep This*),
"Well I didn't think that I could do it and be cred-
ln't really want to do music anymore, until I ran

into Kanye West and we did 'Slow Jamz,' and then after our Ray Charles came out and we did 'Gold Digger,' and I was like, man, this is the time." For more than a decade, Foxx had been trying to gain respect in the music industry, and now that he had success in the entertainment field, he felt it was the right time to release *Unpredictable*. In an interview with Honie Stevens for *Ventana* magazine, Foxx said, "I'd like to say I'm R&B's savior. Whether that's the truth or not, I'm definitely out there with my mic and my shield declaring, 'I am here to save R&B.'"

In just 20 days, the album sold more than one million units. It had to fight for the number 1 spot on the Billboard albums chart, though, because Mary J. Blige's *The Breakthrough* was so immensely popular. *Unpredictable* prevailed, however, and for five weeks it was first on the Billboard charts. Foxx had developed and prepared some of the content of this album on his own; he had also invited a number of his friends who were fellow musicians to guest on his album, including Blige herself, plus Ludacris, Kanye West, and Twista. Foxx is especially proud of "Wish U Were Here," which he wrote for his grandmother, Estelle. Another song, "Heaven," was written for his daughter. With Blige, Foxx sings a duet called "Love Changes," and Foxx and Ludacris team up for the title song, "Unpredictable." Foxx recorded "Extravaganza" with West and "DJ, Play a Love Song" with Twista.

IN HIS OWN WORDS...

In an interview for the *New York Times*, Foxx discussed how important it is to maintain humility and continue to work hard, even after you have had clear successes. He told his interviewer, "When I won the Oscar, I realized that the worst thing I could do was act accordingly. I always think, it's a if you've won the lottery and kept your job: you're rich, but you still wor the post office. You may take an extra 15-minute break, but you don't who you are."

A large portion of the album was recorded from Foxx's home studio, a state-of-the-art room that he recently had built. Working from home enabled him to choose his hours and have a flexible schedule. At other times, Foxx worked from a portable studio on the set of his next movie, *Miami Vice*.

Foxx attributed some of his musical success to his work with Kanye West on two of West's albums; he believed that those songs gave him more credibility in the music industry and helped him record his own popular album. *Rolling Stone* remarked that, "When the album works, it's because of Foxx's easy charm and A-list confidence, which staves off overkill while he's dropping lush, insistent melodies on well-conceived love odes like 'VIP.'" For his work on *Unpredictable*, Foxx received nominations for eight Billboard Music Awards, four Grammy Awards, one Soul Train Music Award, and two American Music Awards. He won Favorite Soul/R&B Male Artist at the American Music Awards.

The American Music Awards, which took place at the Shrine Auditorium in Los Angeles, California, in November 2006, were noteworthy for Foxx. In addition to Foxx winning the award for Favorite Soul/R&B Male Artist, Louise Annette Dixon, Foxx's biological mother, came for the first time. In the past, Foxx had sent his mother invitations to holidays, as well as to his award shows and other events, but she had never shown up.

On this night, his mother chose to come back into his life, and it was an emotional evening for Foxx, who had not seen her in almost 10 years. He performed "Wish U Were Here," the song he wrote for his grandmother from his *Unpredictable* album. Foxx talked to radio and talk-show host Tavis Smiley about how the evening made him feel: "[Louise Annette and I] don't have a relationship that you could . . . say . . . was a mom thing. It was more like here's a lady who I know was important in the process of me getting here. . . . So strange. It was a little different. And my mother still, she's high-faluting." Foxx and his mother did not revive their relationship at that point, but he did remind her that any time she wanted to see him, his door would be open.

SUPPORTING YOUNG NEW TALENT

Whenever he can, Foxx likes to support charities. In April 2006, Jamie Foxx, Antonio "LA" Reid, and Denise Rich were

The Grammys

The Grammy Awards were originally called the Gramophone Awards. In February of each year, the National Academy of Recording Arts and Sciences of the United States presents the awards for outstanding achievements in the record industry. The Grammys are considered the highest music honor a musician can receive in the United States (they are equivalent to the Academy Awards, or Oscars).

The four most prestigious Grammys are Record of the Year, Album of the Year, Song of the Year, and Best New Artist. On December 8, 2006, Jamie Foxx was included in four Grammy nominations:

- Best R&B Performance by a Duo or Group with Vocals for "Love Changes" featuring Mary J. Blige (Sly & the Family Stone, John Legend, and Joss Stone with Van Hunt won the Grammy for "Family Affair")

- Best R&B Album for *Unpredictable* (Mary J. Blige won the Grammy for "*The Breakthrough*)

- Best Rap Performance by a Duo or Group for "Georgia" by Ludacris & Field Mob, featuring Jamie Foxx (Chamillionaire, featuring Krayzie Bone, won the Grammy for "Ridin")

- Best Rap/Sung Collaboration for "Unpredictable" featuring Ludacris (Justin Timberlake, featuring T.I., won the Grammy for "My Love")

At the 49th Annual Grammy Awards show on February 11, 2007, Fo returned to the Staples Center in Los Angeles. He did not win any aw but the four nominations proved that he was gaining a solid reputation music industry.

honored for their philanthropic efforts to support youth arts at the Second Annual Art for Life in Palm Beach, Florida. The event raised about $600,000 to provide access to the arts to disadvantaged youth from Palm Beach County. Foxx believes that it is important to give something back and to help young people find their way in life. He welcomes the opportunity to help enrich the lives of children.

Russell Simmons (the artistic visionary and co-creator of Def Jam) and Kimora Lee Simmons joined the Board of Directors of Rush Philanthropic Arts Foundation to produce the festivities. One of the events was held at Donald Trump's private club Mar-A-Lago in Palm Beach, Florida. Venus Williams, Sammy Sosa, and Star Jones Reynolds were some of the entertainers who were there.

Daman Wayans hosted the 4th Annual BET Awards show, which was broadcast live on June 27, 2006, at the Shrine Auditorium in Los Angeles. The BET Award celebrates African Americans and minorities in music, acting, sports, and other fields of entertainment over the past year. Kanye West won Best Male Hip-Hop Artist. Jamie Foxx was nominated for Best Male R&B Artist (Prince won); in addition, Jamie Foxx (featuring Ludacris) was nominated for Best Duet/Collaboration. Instead, Kanye West (featuring Jamie Foxx) won the award for "Gold Digger," which also won Video of the Year. In addition, Foxx was nominated for Best Actor (Terrence Howard won the award).

MIAMI VICE AND DREAMGIRLS

Foxx appeared in two movies during 2006. After *Jarhead*, he ʼeamed up with Michael Mann for what would be their third ʼect together: a movie version of the 1980s television cop *Miami Vice*, which would appear in theaters in July. Foxx had first discussed the idea in 2002 when they had ʼmmad Ali's birthday party. Mann embraced the pportunity to delve into the world of Miami crime. He focused on the first two seasons, which he thought were the best years of *Miami Vice* for his movie. Foxx also preferred these years—with the fast cars and the tough scenes.

In *Miami Vice*, Foxx played detective Ricardo Tubbs, and Colin Farrell played Sonny Crockett. Mann chose Foxx for the part of Tubbs because, as he told an interviewer, "Jamie is a genius at using mimicry as a means to get to an immediate, spontaneous, truthful place with moment and character. He knows the demeanor that Tubbs should have, and he goes all the way with it." Both Foxx and Farrell trained by observing undercover operations with law enforcement officers. Mann also had the actors take part in undercover situation simulations that taught them how to deal with the physical side of their roles. Their training lasted three months, and Mann thought that the preparation paid off in the final outcome of the film.

Dreamgirls, produced by Dreamworks and Paramount Pictures, hit theaters in December 2006. It was originally a Broadway musical, directed by Michael Bennett, until writer Bill Condon (who had previously directed *Kinsey* in 2004) adapted it for the screen. Condon also directed the movie. Foxx was initially hesitant to sign on because he did not know who else was going to be cast in the film, but when he learned Eddie Murphy was going to take part in it, Foxx changed his mind.

Foxx, in a starring role, played Curtis Taylor Junior, the manager of a trio of soul singers from Chicago. The large cast for this film included Murphy, Danny Glover, third-season *American Idol* finalist Jennifer Hudson, and singer Beyoncé Knowles. Foxx admired Condon and the way he brought the story to the screen. He told an interviewer,

> Bill utilizes the drama of the piece as a catalyst for the music and singing. There's a reason to it all, because the emotional truth of the piece takes you in that direction. Right after "It's All Over," BOOM, you're hit with [Jennifer Hudson's

Based on a Broadway musical of the same name, the movie *Dreamgirls* demanded a cast of actors who could also sing. Foxx played the role of Curtis Taylor Jr., the manager of the girl group, which included (left to right) Beyoncé Knowles, Anika Noni Rose, and Jennifer Hudson.

character] Effie's "And I Am Telling You." It's not just singing for singing's sake. It's storytelling at its most raw and emotional.

Condon brought strong characters and an intriguing story together in this well-made film.

Foxx was once again able to contribute his music abilities to the film by performing the songs "Steppin' to the Bad Side," "Family," "It's All Over," "When I First Saw You," and a second version of "When I First Saw You," which he sang as the end title duet. Movie critics raved about the film's electrifying performances and the fantastic musical numbers. *Entertainment Weekly* called *Dreamgirls* "the rare movie musical with real rapture in it." *Rolling Stone* said, "Foxx is magnetic as the bad guy, showing a grasp of the insecurities that drive the controlling Curtis." *Dreamgirls* won a Golden Globe for Best Motion Picture Musical Comedy and a nomination for Best Ensemble Cast for SAG.

Just a day after *Dreamgirls* opened in theaters, Foxx began a 19-city *Unpredictable* tour. The show would combine stand-up comedy and songs from his last album, *Unpredictable.* Foxx traveled all over the United States in February 2007 to shows in California, Ohio, Wisconsin, Illinois, Missouri, Colorado, New Jersey, Connecticut, Massachusetts, New York, Florida, and Nevada. *American Idol* 2004 winner Fantasia Barrino appeared as the opening act in some of his shows. Some of Foxx's friends who had recorded songs with him joined him for a few of the concerts; at other times, Foxx sang those songs alone. The tour allowed Foxx to work, once again, with live audiences and showcase his many talents.

8

Life on Top

Things were going well for Jamie Foxx. As his fame increased, he accepted more and more television guest appearances over the years. His hosted the popular comedy show *Saturday Night Live*; joined fellow entertainers Angela Bassett, Cuba Gooding Jr., Samuel L. Jackson, Sidney Poitier, Will Smith, John Travolta, and others to celebrate *Muhammad Ali's All-Star 60th Birthday Celebration!*; and was interviewed on *Inside the Actors Studio* by James Lipton.

Foxx also made numerous appearances on major talk shows to promote his movies and albums. These shows included *The Rosie O'Donnell Show*, *The View*, *The Tyra Banks Show*, *The Oprah Winfrey Show*, *Live with Regis and Kelly*, *Late Show with David Letterman*, *The Daily Show*, *Late Night with Conan O'Brien*, and *Ellen: The Ellen DeGeneres Show*. Between rehearsals, film promotions, special guest star appearances, spending time with Corinne, charity work, and keeping up his

After the successes of *Collateral*, *Ray*, *Jarhead*, and *Dreamgirls*, Jamie Foxx was a bona fide star. He is shown here appearing on the September 18, 2007, episode of *The Late Show with Jay Leno*.

music interests, Foxx had little time for anything else, but, as always, he liked to keep busy and push onward.

THE FOXXHOLE

In January 2007, Foxx announced to the public that he would launch a new comedy station on Sirius Satellite Radio called the Foxxhole. Sirius Satellite Radio provides commercial-free programming for its subscribers. The various channels focus on music, news, sports, talk, or comedy. Launched in May 2007, the Foxxhole is a music and comedy station that caters primarily to black listeners. In his position as station chief, Foxx hand-selects much of the music that is played, hosts programs on the shows, and showcases new talent.

One of the regular programs on the show is called *The Jamie Foxx Show*, on which Foxx does his own comedy and talks to special guests from the music, sports, and entertainment world. Foxx uses this radio program as a place to talk and reach out to young people on contemporary topics, such as the importance of speaking up about rap music and the violent images it produces today. Foxx would like to see rappers tone that image down. Recently, he and Jennifer Garner interviewed each other on his show to promote a movie the two appeared in called *The Kingdom*.

Another regular program on the Foxxhole is *The Sheryl Underwood Show*, in which comedian Sheryl Underwood does her own routines, talks about politics, and plays music. *Speedy's Comedy Corner*, starring Speedy, is yet another featured program; Speedy brings Foxx's comedian friends on the show to talk about current world events.

FAMILY LIFE

In 2007, Foxx purchased a 17,000-square-foot (1,579-square-meter) Mediterranean-style mansion on 40 acres in Ventura County, California, for more than $10 million. The mansion, with 10 bedrooms and 12 bathrooms, is far too large for one person, but Foxx did not move in alone. He brought along his stepfather, George Dixon (the man who married Foxx's birth mother after her divorce from Foxx's birth father, Shahid Abdulah), and George's two daughters (Foxx's half sisters), Diondra and Deidra.

Although Foxx's mother and stepfather had since divorced, Foxx had stayed in contact with his half sisters and stepfather over the years. Dixon had served a 10-year prison sentence in Texas. When he was released, Foxx had the parole transferred to California and asked his stepfather to move in with him. Foxx told Josh Young of *Variety*, "[Dixon] never experienced any of the things—the Jamie Foxx things—so when he finally got out [of prison] I just showed him how great life can be. Now we're getting back a lot of lost time."

Foxx's younger half sister, Diondra, has Down syndrome, a genetic disorder that occurs as a result of an extra chromosome.

Diondra is a happy, energetic young woman who shares Foxx's love of comedy. She likes to laugh and tell jokes. Foxx helps to take care of Diondra and ensures that she has what she needs. His other half sister, Deidra, is an accomplished hairdresser who works as Foxx's hairstylist on film sets.

Foxx considers his family, which includes Corinne, George, Diondra, and Deidra, to be of the utmost importance. Just as Foxx wants to be there for them, he knows his family will try to be there for him. In the past, he had friends come and go, depending upon whether or not he had a gig or the type of project he chose. Foxx's family, however, has consistently stood close and supported his ups and downs, his decisions, and his lifestyle.

Foxx lives his life—including work, family, play, and free time—to its very fullest. He loves to host huge parties at his home and he does so with flair. His guest lists have included big-name entertainers like Jay-Z, Whitney Houston, and Brian McKnight. Guests can enjoy guesthouses, an Olympic-size swimming pool, tennis courts, a spa, and a cabana studio on the grounds, as well as a seemingly endless number of rooms inside. The key to a good party, according to Foxx, is good food and fun entertainment. Neither has to be expensive; Foxx has been known to serve fried chicken (a favorite of his) and start a game of basketball. One of the other ways Foxx likes to engage guests is with karaoke.

When Foxx is not hosting a Hollywood party, he likes to listen to music and play games. He keeps a chessboard out and ready to play; he also loves ping-pong and has a table set up in his living room. Foxx once told an interviewer that he would play ping-pong for days straight if he could, and he even keeps his paddle in tip-top shape by tucking it away in a leather case! Foxx also owns a Lamborghini. The first car Foxx ever owned was a 1972 Volkswagen Beetle—clearly, times have changed for Jamie Foxx since his childhood in rural Terrell, Texas.

Despite Foxx's fancy houses and cars, he tries to remain grounded. Knowing that his stardom is not guaranteed to last, he understands the importance of working hard long-term and does not lose sight of the future. Every day he plays his Yamaha baby-grand piano for at least two hours. He loves to play Ray Charles songs ("Let the Good Times Roll" is a favorite) and hip-hop tunes. Foxx's artistic roots are in music, and he nurtures that every day. He also looks for acting projects that have special meaning to him so he can be touched and touch others through the story the film conveys. After winning an Oscar for Best Actor in *Ray*, a significantly compelling film, Foxx has started to see more of these rare gems: well-written screenplays with an ability to expand the audience's awareness and understanding of a particular subject.

FILMS AND POLITICS

In 2007, Foxx created his own production company, called Foxx King Entertainment, with partners Jamie Rucker King and Marcus King. Using his production company, he was the executive producer of *Life Support*, starring Queen Latifah, Carlo Alban, and Darrin Henson. The HBO movie, written (along with Jim McKay and Hannah Weyer) and directed by Nelson George, was a true-life story about a mother who overcame a crack addiction and become a positive role model and an AIDS activist in the black community. Foxx wrote a song for the movie called "Love Brings Change," while he sat at his

IN HIS OWN WORDS...

In an interview for *USA Weekend* with Steven Chean, Foxx talked about how he does not like lazy people. Foxx believes in setting goals and expending energy, working hard and long for your success. He told Chean, "Ain't nothing in this world for free, and it blows my mind how so many fools just don't get that."

piano and watched clips of the movie. He wanted the music to be clean and simple, and he opted for piano music only. The effect was moving. *Life Support* was nominated for two Emmy Awards, including Outstanding Lead Actress in a Miniseries or Movie for Queen Latifah.

Also in 2007, Foxx appeared in Universal Pictures' *The Kingdom*, which opened in theaters in September. Matthew Michael Carnahan wrote the screenplay. Alongside Foxx were actors Jennifer Garner, Jason Bateman, and Chris Cooper. In the political thriller, directed by Peter Berg and produced by Michael Mann and Scott Stuber, Foxx portrays the leader of an FBI team on the hunt for those responsible for a deadly bombing attack on Americans working in Saudi Arabia. Mann knew that Foxx would be a good fit for the role. He told an interviewer, "Jamie can project himself so thoroughly into characters and identities. He's absolutely credible to me as somebody in the FBI—there is a seriousness of intent that these folks have."

Filming *The Kingdom* was intense; Peter Berg wanted shots to be improvised and not overly rehearsed. Berg is an actor as well as a director, so he understood the actors and what they were going through. Berg had even appeared in a couple of movies with Foxx: *The Great White Hype* (1996) and *Collateral* (2004). He had also directed a number of television programs and films, including *Very Bad Things* (1998) and *Friday Night Lights* (2004).

In *The Kingdom*, Berg tried to use material that was relatively unrehearsed, filming when it was fresh and raw, which created a fast-moving, powerful movie. Yet he also wanted the actors to be well trained in small firearms and automatic weapons. Berg had them all in training with real FBI agents in order to learn the skills they would need. In one scene during the film, Foxx was able to bring a taste of his hometown to the movie when Foxx's character, Ronald Fleury, refers to the *Terrell Tribune* newspaper.

Much of the film was shot in the Arizona desert to simulate Saudi Arabia. The actors had to deal with the extreme heat: temperatures were nearly always above 100°F (38°C). Some of *The Kingdom* was also filmed in Abu Dhabi, where Foxx learned more about the Muslim culture. The entire cast was issued a 17-page memo that covered everything they would need to know before they arrived in Abu Dhabi. It suggested that they avoid showing the bottom of one's shoes or feet because doing so is a sign of disrespect, and it mentioned the need to dress modestly.

Basketball and Health Awareness

Jamie Foxx is a natural athlete and a passionate Dallas Cowboys fan. As a child, he played football, tennis, and ran track. Today, Foxx loves a good game of basketball. In one of his homes, he had a court in his backyard so he could play basketball whenever he wanted. He has also participated in charity basketball events when he gets the opportunity.

In 2007, Foxx and Queen Latifah teamed up with National Basketball Association (NBA) Cares to promote testing for the human immunodeficiency virus (HIV). With HIV on the rise in the United States and around the world, these two actors understand how important it is to educate people about HIV and incorporate testing into routine checkups. The actors participated in a public-service ad speaking out about what HIV is and how testing on a regular basis could save a life.

If someone is infected with HIV and it goes untreated, that person will start to make antibodies to fight the infection. A blood test can detect these HIV antibodies; if antibodies are present, the person is HIV-positive. A person has acquired immune deficiency syndrome (AIDS) when his or her immune system is seriously damaged. The HIV virus causes AIDS, which currently has no cure.

Jamie Foxx and Queen Latifah's campaign debuted during Game 5 of the NBA Basketball Finals. The goal of the ad goal was to raise awareness about HIV testing and direct viewers to an online resource (www.testing411.org), developed by NBA Cares, which covers basic information about HIV and gives viewers testing options.

In September 2007, Jamie Foxx was honored with a star on
the Hollywood Walk of Fame in Los Angeles. He accepted the
award with his daughter, Corinne, by his side, and thanked
his late grandmother, Estelle Talley.

Once in Abu Dhabi, Foxx and the cast were set up in the
Emirates Palace Hotel, a 247-acre luxurious resort, where parts
of the movie were also filmed. Foxx found the gold-leaf walls,

marble corridors, and 1,000-piece Swarovski crystal chandeliers a bit daunting, yet it was a very pleasurable place to spend time. He even brought his family along.

The response to *The Kingdom* was lukewarm. Critics thought that, although there were a few good action sequences, most of the action was too bloody and over-the-top. It lacked smart dialogue and plot; instead, the film relied on formulaic Hollywood thriller scenes without much success. Some reviewers, however, did have positive things to say about Foxx's role in the movie. The *San Francisco Chronicle* noted, "Foxx, almost from film to film, continues to strengthen and deepen as a leading man." The *Denver Post* said, "[Foxx] carries the film's moral hopes and ambitions like a seasoned athlete."

In September, Jamie Foxx earned a star on the Hollywood Walk of Fame. The dedication ceremony took place on September 14, and Foxx was there with his daughter, Corinne. The Walk of Fame honors people who have made significant contributions in the entertainment industry through radio, television, motion pictures, recording, and live performance. Upon accepting the honor, Foxx again gave thanks to his grandmother, Estelle Talley, when he said, "My grandmother's got to be spreading her wings and flying around in heaven, just so happy."

On September 18, an all-star lineup participated in a three-hour variety show called the "Dream Concert," with proceeds going to the construction of a memorial honoring Dr. Martin Luther King Jr., to be built on the National Mall in Washington, D.C. The show, appearing in Radio City Music Hall in New York City, boasted big-name performers, including Stevie Wonder and Aretha Franklin. Foxx's friend Ludacris sang "Lost Without You." Foxx was one of many host committee members, each of whom gave a short speech during the evening. Other members included Ben Affleck, Muhammad Ali, Angela Bassett, Cuba Gooding Jr., Magic Johnson, Michael

Jordan, Shaquille O'Neal, LaDainian Tomlinson, and Kerry Washington.

Foxx has never been one to shy away from controversial topics, which includes politics. He defended his friend Kanye West when West openly criticized President George Bush. Foxx did not think President Bush had handled Hurricane Katrina appropriately and he did not mind saying so. In September 2007, Foxx told Miki Turner of MSNBC, "I'm supporting Barack Obama and if by chance he doesn't win, I will support whoever the Democratic candidate is." Then, in October, Foxx met Illinois senator Barack Obama when Obama was in Los Angeles. Obama spoke to a group about his presidential campaign for 2008 and to recruit volunteers to appear in campaign spots. Jamie Foxx donated $2,300 to the Obama campaign. Other celebrities who have donated to the campaign include Will Smith, Tom Hanks, and Jodie Foster.

In November 2007, Foxx appeared at the 41st Annual Country Music Awards (CMA) to perform with Rascal Flatts. The awards show was held at the Sommet Center in Nashville, Tennessee. Foxx sang "She Goes All the Way," which he recorded with the band for their album *Still Feels Good*. Foxx had known Gary LeVox, the lead guitarist of Rascal Flatts, since the late 1990s. At that time, the two musicians had briefly roomed together after Foxx's manager, Marcus King, introduced them. Foxx and LeVox were reunited in 2007 when they met at the 2007 Grammy Awards. Since the Grammies, Foxx and LeVox have stayed in touch.

On December 23, 2007, Jamie Foxx—along with Ben Stiller (who played the voice of "Stiller the Elf"), Alicia Keys, Jennifer Hudson, Kevin James, and other celebrities—joined Elmo to count down the days to Christmas on *Elmo's Christmas Countdown*. The one-hour special costarred Sesame Street characters Big Bird, Grover, Oscar, Count von Count, and Snuffleupagus.

9

Looking Forward

Where does Jamie Foxx go from here? Fans recently nominated Foxx for a People's Choice Award for Favorite Leading Man. The 34th Annual People's Choice Awards aired live on January 8, 2008, and were hosted by Queen Latifah. Foxx lost to Joaquin Phoenix, but it did not slow Foxx down. He will continue to do what he does best, which is to entertain audiences around the world via stand-up comedy, music, radio, and film. Foxx continually works with his managers, Jamie Rucker King and Marcus King, to ensure that he has an opportunity to connect with high-quality, meaningful scripts.

Fans of Jamie Foxx can keep up-to-date with his music ventures, television appearances, movie synopses, and radio news by visiting his Web site at www.jamiefoxx.com. The site, launched on December 5, 2005, also offers a community blog where fans can discuss an array of topics surrounding Foxx, such as news about his latest nominations and awards, wallpaper downloads, and photos. Fans can also listen to excerpts from his albums and news about upcoming projects. For example, fans who visited the site knew that *The Kingdom* was available to own on DVD (with extras, including deleted scenes and the "making of" documentaries) beginning December 26, 2007.

UPCOMING PROJECTS AND THE WRITERS' STRIKE

In October 2007, Foxx announced he had signed on with DreamWorks to appear in the movie *The Zebra Murders: A Season of Killing, Racial Madness, and Civil Rights*. Foxx's production company, Foxx King Entertainment, will produce the film, along with production company Plan B (run by Brad Pitt and Dede Gardner). The movie is based on a book by Prentice Earl Sanders and Bennett Cohen. Matthew Michael Carnahan, who also wrote the screenplay for *The Kingdom*, will adapt the book to the screen.

In the film, Foxx will play Sanders, one of two black police detectives who cracked the case on a series of murders in San Francisco. While he worked on the case, Sanders had faced a great deal of harassment within the police department, but he overcame the discrimination and became San Francisco's first black chief of police. *The Zebra Murders* is tentatively scheduled to appear in theaters in the year 2010.

In November 2007, Foxx King Entertainment teamed up with MTV and VH1 to produce a reality show called *From Gs to Gents*, which will follow a group of men who compete to become the perfect gentleman. Throughout the show, the men will receive social makeovers to help turn them into gentlemen. Foxx signed a two-year business agreement with MTV and VH1 for the show. He, along with his production partners Jamie Rucker King and Marcus King, will develop, produce, and consult on unscripted projects for MTV and VH1.

Foxx's new R&B album, called *Man's Intuition*, is slated to be in stores for Christmas 2008. This will be Foxx's third album, which he describes as a series of songs that tells a story about what women want from men. Although Foxx considers himself to be a ladies' man who can romance a woman and sweep her off her feet, he also feels mystified by them. He uses his music to sort through some of these jumbled feelings.

Foxx also has a movie planned for 2008. In *The Soloist*, written by Susannah Grant, Foxx worked with award-winning British director Joe Wright for the first time. Wright's previous directorial accomplishments include a television miniseries, *Charles II: The Power and the Passion* (2003), as well as films *Pride and Prejudice* (2005) and the critically-acclaimed *Atonement* (2007).

Foxx has a starring role in the movie, which is based on the true story of Nathaniel Anthony Ayers, who developed schizophrenia during his second year at the Juilliard School. As a result of his psychological disorder, Ayers ended up homeless and living underneath a Los Angeles freeway. During the day, he performs on his violin and cello on the streets of downtown Los Angeles; he dreams of one day playing at Walt Disney Concert Hall. Ayers plays his instruments in order to drown out the numerous voices he hears in his head, which is a symptom of schizophrenia. Steve Lopez, a columnist from the *Los Angeles Times*, heard Ayers play one day and struck up a conversation with him. As a result of this chance meeting, Lopez wrote a series of articles for the newspaper that tell Ayers's story.

To prepare for his role as Nathaniel Ayers, Foxx learned to play the cello from Ben Hong, assistant principal cello player with the Los Angeles Philharmonic. Although the film will use Hong's music and not Foxx's, Foxx still needed to learn the basics of the instrument to accurately portray a performance on screen. He also learned to play the violin. Costarring with Foxx is Robert Downey Jr., as Steve Lopez.

Unfortunately, all of Foxx's upcoming movie projects were delayed by the Writers Guild strike against the Alliance of

Foxx has proven his unstoppable star power and box-office draw, thus earning the ability to pick and choose which projects he participates in. In 2008, he was slated to begin filming a new movie, though the 2007–2008 writers' strike delayed production.

Motion Picture and Television Producers, which started on November 5, 2007 and concluded on February 12, 2008. The writers, whose contracts ran out at the end of October, were asking for a pay increase for movies and television shows released on DVD, as well as more royalty money from movies and television shows distributed on the Internet.

The most serious immediate casualties that resulted from the Hollywood writers' strike were the late-night talk shows; because they are written about current events, they had to stop new episodes. Daytime daily talk shows were also hit hard. The next group of programs to be affected were the sitcoms and dramas that did not have their full seasons written ahead of time. Once the scripts for the written episodes had aired, the producers had nothing to put on television. Then, movie companies started to feel the effects of the writers' strike. Directors Oliver Stone and Ron Howard both announced that they were putting their upcoming movies on hold because their scripts were not ready.

Foxx's television and movie projects were not greatly delayed by the strike, but if they had been, this ambitious celebrity would probably have found other types of projects with which to fill his time. Although as an actor, Foxx needs a writer's script, his success as a comedian, songwriter, and musician provides him with several creative outlets.

THE SOUTHERN GENTLEMAN

Jamie Foxx has never allowed life to pass him by, and he has not chosen to sit back and relax when things are going especially well. Foxx takes chances. He has taken on stand-up comedy, singing, and acting, as well as started a satellite radio station and a production company. Challenges do not intimidate Foxx; indeed, they inspire him. Foxx is confident and self-directed, and, more important, he is not afraid to fail. If he does stumble, he gets right back into the game and tries that much harder. Foxx sets his sights high and does not shy away from the hard work needed to get there.

From his rural, small-town upbringing, Jamie Foxx learned from his grandmother, Estelle Talley, how to stand up tall, keep his shoulders back, and hold his head high. She wanted to see him rise above the discrimination and the segregation and to create a happy, enriched, successful life for himself. Jamie Foxx has done just that.

SELECTED WORKS AND AWARDS

FILMS

1992 *Toys*

1996 *The Truth About Cats and Dogs*

1996 *The Great White Hype*

1997 *Booty Call*

1998 *The Players Club*

1999 *Held Up*

1999 *Any Given Sunday*

2000 *Bait*

2001 *Ali*

2003 *Shade*

2004 *Breakin' All the Rules*

2004 *Collateral*

2004 *Ray*

2005 *Stealth*

2005 *Jarhead*

2006 *Miami Vice*

2006 *Dreamgirls*

2007 *The Kingdom*

2008 *The Soloist* (in production)

TELEVISION/VIDEOS

1991–1994 *In Living Color*

1992–1993 *Roc*

1993 *Jamie Foxx: Straight From the Foxxhole*

1996 *C-Bear and Jamal* (voice)

1996   *Hangin' With Mr. Cooper*

1996   *Moesha*

1996–2001   *The Jamie Foxx Show*

2002   *Jamie Foxx: I Might Need Security*

2003   *Jamie Foxx Unleashed: Lost, Stolen and Leaked!*

2004   *Redemption: The Stan Tookie Williams Story*

2004   *Chappelle's Show*

AWARDS

1998   Image Award (outstanding lead actor in a comedy series) for *The Jamie Foxx Show*.

2002   Image Award (outstanding supporting actor in a motion picture) for *Ali*. Black Reel Award (theatrical—best supporting actor) for *Ali*.

2004   Washington DC Area Film Critics Association Awards (best actor) for *Ray* and (best supporting actor) for *Collateral*. Southeastern Film Critics Association Award (best actor) for *Ray*. Seattle Film Critics Award (best actor) for *Ray*. Phoenix Film Critics Society Award (best performance by an actor in a leading role) for *Ray*. National Board of Review, USA Award (best actor) for *Ray*. Hollywood Film Festival (breakthrough actor). Florida Film Critics Circle Award (best actor) for *Ray*. Boston Society of Film Critics Award (best actor) for *Ray*.

2005   Vancouver Film Critics Circle Award (best actor) for *Ray*. Screen Actors Guild Award (outstanding performance by a male actor in a leading role) for *Ray*. Golden Satellite Award (best actor in a motion picture, comedy, or musical) for *Ray* and (best actor in a miniseries or a motion picture made for television) for *Redemption: The Stan Tookie Williams Story*. Prism Award (performance in a feature film) for *Ray*. National Society of Film

Critics Award (best actor) for *Ray*. MovieGuide Grace Award (most inspiring television acting) for *Redemption: The Stan Tookie Williams Story*. London Critics Circle Film ALFS Award (actor of the year) for *Ray*. Las Vegas Film Critics Society Sierra Award (best actor) for *Ray*. Kansas City Film Critics Circle Award (best actor) for *Ray*. Image Award (outstanding actor in a television movie, miniseries, or dramatic special) for *Redemption: The Stan Tookie Williams Story* and (outstanding actor in a motion picture) for *Ray*. Golden Globe (best performance by an actor in a motion picture—musical or comedy) for *Ray*. Broadcast Film Critics Association Award (best actor) for *Ray*. Black Reel Award (best supporting actor) for *Collateral*, (best actor, network/cable television) for *Redemption: The Stan Tookie Williams Story*, and (best actor, drama) for *Ray*. BET Award (best actor) for *Ray*. BAFTA Film Award (best performance by an actor in a leading role) for *Ray*. Academy Oscar Award (best performance by an actor in a leading role) for *Ray*.

2006   American Music Award (favorite soul/R&B male artist); BET Award (Video of the Year) for "Gold Digger."

1967 Eric Marlon Bishop is born on December 13 in Terrell, Texas.

1986 Bishop graduates from Terrell High School in June.

1986–1988 Bishop studies classical piano at San Diego's United States International University.

1989 Bishop changes name to Jamie Foxx while on comedy circuit.

1991 Foxx enters and wins the Bay Area Black Comedy Competition and Festival (BABCCF).

1991–1994 Foxx has role on the television comedy-sketch show *In Living Color*.

1993 Foxx stars in his own comedy special, *Jamie Foxx: Straight From the Foxxhole*.

1994 Foxx's debut R&B album, *Peep This*, released by Fox Records.

1995 Foxx's daughter, Corinne, is born.

1996–2001 Foxx stars in *The Jamie Foxx Show*, which he also co-created and executive-produced, on the WB.

1998 Foxx coproduces first *Jamie Foxx Presents Laffapalooza!*

1999 Foxx appears in his breakout film, *Any Given Sunday*.

2001 He appears in *Ali*.

2003 Releases smash-hit single, "Slow Jamz," with Kanye West and Twista.

2004 Appears in *Redemption: The Stan Tookie Williams Story* on FX; plays Max in *Collateral*; stars as Ray Charles in *Ray*.

2005 Records "Gold Digger" with Kanye West and Twista; wins Academy Award for Best Actor for his performance in *Ray*; releases his second album, *Unpredictable*.

2006 Appears in *Dreamgirls*.

2007 Announces the launching of comedy channel The Foxxhole on Sirius Satellite Radio; stars in the film *The Kingdom.*

2008 *The Soloist* is set to premiere in November.

Chean, Steven. "Music Man," USAWeekend.com. Available online. URL: www.usaweekend.com/04_issues/041031/041031jamie_foxx.html. October 31, 2004.

Dougherty, Terri. *Jamie Foxx*. People in the News. Farmington Hills, Mich.: Lucent Books/Gale Group, 2006.

Horn, Geoffrey. *Jamie Foxx*. Today's Superstars: Entertainment Series. Strongsville, Ohio: Gareth Stevens, 2005.

Oprah. "Oprah Talks to Jamie Foxx." *O, The Oprah Magazine*, December 2005.

Orr, Tamra B. *Jamie Foxx*. A Blue Banner Biography. Hockessin, Dela.: Mitchell Lane, 2006.

WEB SITES

"21st Century Foxx," Guardian.co.uk
http://film.guardian.co.uk/interview/interview-pages/0,,1355828,00.html

"*Any Given Sunday* Official Site"
http://anygivensunday.warnerbros.com

"*Dreamgirls* Official Site"
www.dreamgirlsmovie.com

"Jamie Foxx," The Internet Movie Database
www.imdb.com/name/nm0004937

"The Official Jamie Foxx Site"
www.jamiefoxx.com

"The Official Ray Charles Site"
www.raycharles.com

"Ray: An Interview with Jamie Foxx," Blackfilm.com
http://www.blackfilm.com/20041022/features/jamiefoxx.shtml

"*Ray* Official Site"
www.raymovie.com

PAGE

Index

About the Author

Anne M. Todd has a Bachelor of Arts degree in English and American Indian Studies from the University of Minnesota. She has written more than 20 nonfiction children's books, including biographies on American Indians, political leaders, and entertainers. Todd is also the author of the following Chelsea House books: *Roger Maris*, from the Baseball Superstars series, *Mohandas Gandhi*, from the Spiritual Leaders and Thinkers series, *Chris Rock*, from the Black Americans of Achievement, Legacy Edition series, and *Vera Wang*, from the Asian Americans of Achievement series. Todd lives in Prior Lake, Minnesota, with her husband, Sean, and three sons, Spencer, William, and Henry.